RELOCATING THE PERSONAL

Relocating the Personal

A Critical Writing Pedagogy

BARBARA KAMLER

With a Foreword by Michelle Fine

STATE UNIVERSITY OF NEW YORK PRESS

Cover art, (Scroll, 1999) by Aloma Triester. Courtesy of the artist.

Published by
State University of New York Press, Albany

For information, address State University of New York Press,
State University Plaza, Albany, NY 12246

Production by Marilyn P. Semerad
Marketing by Dana E. Yanulavich

Library of Congress Cataloging-in-Publication Data

Kamler, Barbara.
    Relocating the personal : a critical writing pedagogy / Barbara Kamler ; with a
foreword by Michelle Fine.
        p.   cm.
    Includes bibliographical references and index.
    ISBN 0-7914-4811-8 (alk. paper) — ISBN 0-7914-4812-6 (pbk. : alk. paper)
    1. English language—Rhetoric—Study and teaching. 2. Interdisciplinary approach in
education. 3. Creative writing—Study and teaching. 4. Critical pedagogy. 5.
Autobiography. I. Title.

PE1404.K36 2001
808'.042—dc21   00-026528
                    10   9   8   7   6   5   4   3   2   1

To Jeanne Heidenreich Kamler

My first writing teacher

Contents

Foreword   *ix*

Preface   *xiii*

Chapter One   **SPACE, TIME, EMBODIED TEXTS** *1*

Chapter Two   **RELOCATING VOICE AND TRANSFORMATION** *35*

Chapter Three   **STORIES OF AGEING** *55*

Chapter Four   **WHO SAID ARGUMENTATIVE WRITING ISN'T PERSONAL?** *79*

Chapter Five   **CRITICAL SPACES FOR LEARNING TO TEACH WRITING** *109*

Chapter Six   **LANGUAGE, GENDER, WRITING** *137*

Chapter Seven   **THE POLITICS OF THE PERSONAL: NEW METAPHORS, NEW PRACTICES** *171*

Bibliography *187*

Index *203*

Foreword

❖

We may look back on this moment in history as the days of educational redlining: the exiling of the public from public education, the extraction of joy and the novelty of academic surprises from the teaching experience, the smotherings of intellectual creativity and curiosity in the name of 'standards'. Indeed, within the neoliberal assault on public education, 'standards' and access sit in a perverse seesaw. The former is presumably on the rise as the latter falls painfully on the backs of the poor and working class. In the United States redlining takes the form of anti–Affirmative Action policies, a retreat from remediation, heightened tuition rates, reduced financial aid, welfare 'reform' whereby women must accept low-level jobs rather than pursue higher education and a 'standards' movement by which the only ones held accountable are poor and working class youth and young adults increasingly shut out of higher education. In the midst of a rising elitism within the academy, Barbara Kamler invites readers to remember joy and to consider a democratizing of education; that is, she argues for the teaching of writing as a political project in schools and communities.

In *Relocating the Personal: A Critical Writing Pedagogy*, Kamler introduces us to writers in unsuspecting bodies— ageing women, 60 to 90, with stories and more stories to tell; a sixteen-year-old 'failed writer'; a set of undergraduate teacher education students; and postgraduate Master's students, engaged in off-campus distance learning. We learn about the delicate practice of writing pedagogy: the power of working with multiple frameworks, the joys of a pedagogy that is at once collective and deconstructive, the struggle to theorise 'personal experience—[and] relocate [that] experience within broader social, cultural and political contexts of production'.

Crafting a text on writing pedagogy, Kamler produces a book on cultural histories of ordinary peoples and their schools. Encouraging her students to be coresearchers, together they carve 'risky territories' in which they refuse to position language as 'neutral communication' and insist, instead, upon interrogating the ideological and strategic moves of schooling. They write to know, and they revise to know again, culturally, as a sea of humans making collective meanings of the shifting structures, formations, ideologies and geographies of their lives.

With *Relocating the Personal*, Barbara Kamler offers readers two gifts. The first is a rich collection of critical writings, by so many different kinds of students, writing from so many different sites for education. Across these works, Kamler reveals teaching as delicate and prodding, respectful and nudging, predictable and fundamentally surprising. Relations of teaching and learning grow in schools, communities, around dining-room tables and within adult education writing groups. Kamler's second gift is a text on critical pedagogy in which she is herself explicit and self-critical, instructive and generous about the teaching of writing. In ways deeply feminist and poststructuralist, Kamler details how she works with students to extract cultural texts from under the stubborn lamination of the personal story. Carefully sculpting cultural stories from the clay of what seems so personal, Kamler dares to enter the terrain of pain, oppression, pleasure, tragedy, joy and loss. With grace and respect, she creates contexts in which students migrate from that which seems so private back into historic and political contexts, embroidering a cultural frame around often buried stories that feel so unique, authentic and distinctly one's own.

In the task of 'relocating the personal', Barbara Kamler rewrites social history, writing pedagogy and adult psychology. She borrows delicately from the 'personal closet', stories of power, gender, 'failure', the body, ageing, sexuality and anxiety. Renouncing the 'true, inner voice', out of the closet tumble multiple stories revealing what she calls 'collective biographies' of ideology, subversion, resistance and cultural reproduction.

Reading this text we remember the power and delights of educating with rather than for or despite; we recognize the many places in which learning flourishes, within and well beyond schools; we witness the strength acquired and exercised in writing and writing again; and we remember the rush of telling stories, not merely for personal meaning, but for social significance. Hesitant always to generalize from her cases, Kamler provides modestly a foundation for resuscitating a global conversation about critical pedagogy across generations and place. As in the past, those of us in the United States and Europe may look to Australia and New Zealand for pedagogical lights and courage. For all of that and more, we are, again, grateful.

MICHELLE FINE
CUNY Graduate School and University Center

Preface

❖

BARBARA CAN'T WRITE. NEW JERSEY, 1962–1965

I am not a writer. I cannot write. I am 15 years old, 16 years old, 17 years old. I am convinced of this. This is what I have learned most powerfully from my schooling. Fear and a strong sense of inadequacy as a writer. I am good at grammar lessons and spelling. I am the tallest girl in the class and at the end of the spelling bee I am still standing. Victorious. But essays bewilder me. Each time I am assigned an essay I panic. I read and reread, make notes and agonise. I have no idea what to write or how to get started. I find no help in advice that tells me to write a plan first and follow it. When teachers require me to submit the plan, I first write the essay and do the plan later. How else do I know what I am going to say? But I feel this is cheating—further evidence of my failure to get it right. Never does it occur to me there may be something wrong with the advice.

I am overwhelmed by the pressure to get it right. I am a perfectionist and I know the pathetic whimpering that lands on my page for what it is, pathetic. And so inevitably I find myself starring in a scene which goes like this. The setting is the kitchen table. The paper is due the next day. It is getting later and later, and my mother is in the kitchen. She may be reading the paper or finishing *The New York Times* crossword as she smokes. I sit at the table and start to cry. I don't know what to write. And so my mother, once a teacher herself, begins to ask me questions. What is the essay about? What do I know about the topic? Well could I say . . . ? and how about . . . ? Her words are long gone but as she speaks I write her words down—as many as I can. Later I fill in the gaps, make the links. And little by little the essay takes shape. I know that if I sit there long enough and cry long enough, she will write the essay for me and alleviate the fear that imprisons my words.

These many years later it's the gold-sprinkled Formica table I remember, the hum of the dishwasher, and my mother's soft crooning, 'Could you say this and that?' I came to believe my mother wrote my essays. I had no notion then of the legitimacy of collaboration or of scaffolding the writing of the less experienced. My first year at university, a five-hour drive from my home, I read George Orwell's *On Shooting an Elephant* and was required to write a one-page essay. I stayed up all night. I cried and ate and submitted a pathetic effort to my tutor at my Saturday 8:00 A.M. class. And failed. The tortured freshman failed her first essay. Ever. Confirmation that she cannot write without her mother.

Viewing the Formica table in New Jersey from the table where I now sit, it comes as something of a surprise to realise I have been sitting at this table for a lifetime: as a teacher with less experienced writers like my son and my students (undergraduate, Master's, PhD); as an editor with colleagues and friends whose texts I treat as clay, as possibility; as a writer talking to mentors about my own writing. The tables change from Formica to wood veneer, to teak, to white polyethylene—but the conversations at these tables are always imbued with a pleasure I suddenly understand I learned from sitting with my mother. This woman who sat at the kitchen table in clouds of smoke cajoling and coaxing me, whose no-nonsense assumption that I would write has written into my body the pleasure of that sociality, the interruption of fear—the transformation of a solitary and lonely act into a shared performance.

Were my mother alive she would smile at the irony of her daughter writing a book on teaching writing. The daughter who knew she couldn't write. My passion as a writing teacher finds its genesis in that failure—and in the help of those teachers who eventually showed me I could write.

CHAPTER ONE

Space, Time, Embodied Texts

---------------- ❖ ----------------

As I begin to map the territory of knowledge and desire I call this book, I am taken by the idea of relocation and the questions it raises. The subject of this book is writing, but the subject is also the personal. What might it mean to relocate the personal when issues of writing and self are so closely entwined?

The notion of relocation implies a dissatisfaction—a desire to move elsewhere from somewhere. I am dissatisfied with the way the personal is treated in school writing as a space of confession, a telling of inner truth. I am also dissatisfied with current competency-based moves to eradicate the personal from school writing altogether and focus on the more functional genres students need to master in the 'real world'. I wish to assert the importance of working with the writer's personal experience but differently—by relocating the personal—theoretically and pedagogically—in a way that allows a more critical engagement with experience.

I begin this relocation by mapping a set of places—where I have been, where I now stand, where I wish to go. This chapter locates my understandings of a critical writing pedagogy in 'the personal'—in my life stories as these have unfolded over the past thirty years. I attempt, however, not to tell my story as a sequentially, unfolding realist tale, a modernist history of cause and effect. I want to resist constructing

1

my academic work, or anyone's academic work, as a seamless set of paradigmatic shifts—from process to genre to poststructuralism. I want to resist, as well, conversion narratives, where the teacher/scholar 'sees the light', disavows the past and proclaims the foolishness of her ways.

Instead, I engage in two simultaneous moves: to spatialise the conventional narrative and to locate the autobiographical in its social and cultural landscape. I turn to Edward Soja (1989), a postmodern geographer, to help me with this mapping—as 'a geography of simultaneous relations and meanings that are tied together by a spatial rather than a temporal logic' (1989:1)—and to poststructuralist feminist educators Linda Brodkey and Bronwyn Davies, for their work on autoethnography and cultural biography, respectively.

Soja argues that time and history have occupied a privileged position in both social life and social theory and that it may be space more than time that now needs attention. This requires not simply a metaphorical move 'that makes geography matter as much as history', but a deconstruction and reconstitution of our thinking—the construction of 'a politicised spatial consciousness' (Soja 1989:75) where 'space cannot be dealt with as if it were merely a passive, abstract arena on which things happen' (Keith and Pile 1993:2).

For Soja, the spaces where we live, work and write are never neutral.

> We must be insistently aware of how space can be made to hide consequences from us, how relations of power and discipline are inscribed into the apparently innocent spatiality of social life, how human geographies become filled with politics and ideology. (Soja 1989:6)

A discussion of writing pedagogies—the way these 'become filled with politics and ideology'—can be productively framed by spatial metaphors—highlighting connections across territories and paradigms as well as disjunctures. In this book I argue for bringing together a variety of writing pedagogies that cross boundaries—including process and genre-based approaches, as these have been developed in Australia, with elements of poststructural theory. I see this project as more than banal eclecticism or a simple adding of one paradigm to another. There is a history, a development of these paradigms over time which must be acknowledged—but there is also a spatial dimension which interacts with my own experience in educational sites. This spatiality is socially produced, and like society itself, exists in both substantial forms (concrete spatialities) and as a set of relations between individuals and groups, 'an embodiment and medium of social life itself' (Soja 1989:120).

Because this is a book about writing and the self, I am interested in how we might construct what Brodkey, in her reading of Soja, calls 'historicised spaces inhabited by the human body'. Brodkey sees the self, the 'I', in theoretical terms as a postmodern site which

> embodies relations between actually lived and socially produced spaces: in empirical terms, the 'I' is a site whose memories of lived experiences of social and historical spaces are recounted as narratives of personal experience; in practical terms, everyone is an 'I Site' by definition and either already can or may well wish to explore in writing the historicised spaces of their personal narratives. (Brodkey 1996b:18)

To create a critical, spatial perspective in narrative presents both a linguistic and theoretical challenge. Soja argues for tampering 'with the familiar modalities of time, to shake up the normal flow of the linear text' (1989:1). 'All that we can do is re-collect and creatively juxtapose, experimenting with assertions and insertions of the spatial against the prevailing grain of time' (1989:2). Brodkey and Davies argue for relocating personal experience in a cultural frame—so that writing about the self becomes an invitation to identify, analyse and critique, to understand the discursive practices that construct the sense of self—which in turn offer possibilities for social change.

Brodkey uses the term *autoethnography*, coined by Françoise Lionnet to describe a genre which 'opens up a space of resistance between the individual (auto–) and the collective (–ethno–) where the writing (–graphy) of singularity cannot be foreclosed' (1990:391). While autoethnographies resemble personal narratives in that they concern the writer's life, they differ to the extent that personal histories are grounded in cultural analysis and criticism. Autoethnographies, according to Brodkey, 'are produced by people who acknowledge their multiple affiliations and realise that they are strategically poised to interrupt the negative effects of what passes for common sense' (1996b:28).

In *Writing on the Bias* (1994), Brodkey's elegant autoethnographic narrative of childhood encounters with literacy, she disrupts commonsense notions that equate successful writing with learning sets of rules and conventions (spelling, grammar, punctuation). Brodkey represents herself as a working-class child, triumphantly marching down the steps of the public library or interviewing her neighbourhood informants in exchange for conversation and food. Through the pleasurable detail of her narrative, she argues that her own success as a writer owes more to the intellectual practices she learned in her working-class home and neighbourhood than to her middle-class schooling's attention to correctness.

Like Brodkey, Davies' attraction to autobiographical writing lies in the potential for social change as well as the pleasure and insights that may accrue to the writer. While Brodkey's metaphor for autobiographical writing is research—autoethnographies are grounded in data collected from 'interviews with the self', memories are treated as 'data' which are discussed, analysed—Davies' metaphor is story, where the individual story (autobiography) is located/shaped by the cultural storylines that frame it.

Davies (1994) uses the term 'collective biography' to refer to stories which move beyond a statement about the particular individual who wrote the story to a revelation of the social and discursive processes through which we become individuals. Basing her work on Frigga Haug's (1987) memory work, Davies' focus is more on textual strategy than text—

on developing a deconstructive process of reading and analysing autobiographical stories in order to make visible that which is usually taken for granted. Through this process, she argues, writers can 'examine the construction of their own biography as something at the same time experienced as personal and their own—woven out of their body/minds—and yet visibly made out of, even determined by, materials and practices not originating from them' (Davies 1992:83–4).

This kind of cultural analysis alerts writers to the narrative possibilities of their experience—reminding the reader that what 'we call personal experience is a narrative production' (Brodkey 1994:210). When we make space as crucial a component of that production as time, what results are embodied texts, where the body (sexed, gendered, racialised, classed) cannot be written out or ignored, where the body insists on occupying some space and will not be silenced. What results is an understanding of text as processual—as a process of making which is profoundly embodied and disciplined, subject to all kinds of policy, institutional, private and power relationships—'always narrative, dialogic and rhetorical' (Threadgold 1997:22). There is pleasure in writing oneself as an embodied self—in moving across a terrain of landscapes, geographical relocations and scholarly terrains. There are also dangers of getting lost in the pleasure of the journey, losing sight of what we're telling or why we're trying to map these locations.

LIFE AS RELOCATION

The power of spatial metaphors to reshape writing and self is profound. Once I understand relocation as an embodied social and political act, the stories I've told of my life and work are suddenly transfigured by metaphors of movement and place—as dislocations and relocations across the northern and southern hemispheres. Such is the power of a new metaphor to reframe old stories. Critical discourses such as poststructuralism, Pam Gilbert (1993a) argues, allow us to make spaces outside dominant paradigms where different stories can be made and read. By constructing 'layers of stories, one upon the other and one beside the other . . . the stories construct a new discursive field upon which we can draw as we search for different ways to talk and write' (1993a:4).

The stories my family tell construct me as a timid child who never wanted to leave the space called home, who cried inconsolably on her first day at school and the weeks following, who every Sunday night crept into her mother's bed for comfort and the hope she might be allowed to stay home on Monday. The same child, they say, sobbed when her parents sent her to summer camp, terrified of being sent away from home to have fun with strangers. While other middle-class children seemed gleeful to escape their parents, small Barbara was devastated to leave her mother. So she cried. She cried on the bus and she cried in her bunk each night. Until she found girlfriends, water skiing, hikes, boys, slow dancing, Johnny Matthis and a less stressful set of social class relations in this new location. This was a world less regulated by country club affiliations and the cruel exclusions of the middle-class community where she grew up wondering what she had to do to be popular. It was a space that allowed her to construct new subjectivities outside the discourses of exclusion that dominated the home place.

This same child—this Barbara—had a late adolescence. When mothers bemoaned the insolence of their white teenage middle–class daughters, her mother smiled Madonna–like and boasted that she and Barbara talked about everything. So it came as somewhat of a shock when at age 23 this Barbara left home in a big way. She met *that man* at New York University—in the days of radical street politics and Vietnam moratoriums—and she moved in with him. Later, she married and moved to Australia for two years. That was in 1972, the Nixon years, when U.S. troops invaded Cambodia and killed students on the campus of Kent Sate University. Twenty-eight years later she still lives in Australia, although she never decided to stay.

Her relocation to Australia has been a site of controversy and despair for her family. She was raised in a culture that places a premium on home—on the cultural affiliation and parental devotion of its children. Jewish girls rarely go so far away from home and when they do, they rarely stay away so long. Her grandmother Sophie, of course, did just that at age 16. The eldest of nine children, Sophie begged her father's mother for passage to the United States and with her brother, Myer, travelled by boat in what she called 'stowage class'—with the cargo. She left behind Poland, her five sisters and brothers and her mother, pregnant with twins, to make her way to the land of opportunity—where she bluffed her way into a job and learned to make boas from wild, pink ostrich feathers.

The stories Sophie told of relocation in that wave of migration during the 1890s were Horatio Alger tales of courage and triumph. She worked, married, brought her mother and seven brothers and sisters to America, raised her own family, built a solid family business with her husband. But when her granddaughter Barbara migrated to Australia, left the civilised and modern land of opportunity to go to that place down under, she despaired. There was no persecution, no deprivation, no need. Discourses of survival and opportunity were not available for her to produce a reading of her granddaughter's journey as other than self-indulgent and unnecessary. And to be alone. On each return visit her grandmother cried, 'I think of you there so alone—without your family. Come back Barbara. No one should be so alone'.

So this Barbara is a traveller—a relocated scholar—situated somewhere between the United States and Australia—maintaining citizenship in one and residence in the other. She reads and writes and publishes and does research in communities that cross continents. The traces of these locations are everywhere evident in the stories that follow—in the theoretical borrowings—in the desire to locate herself within an intersecting set of theories, practices, continents that constitute her understanding of writing and writing pedagogy.

This kind of geographical work is timely given the current and growing interest in 'the personal', 'the self' and 'the autobiographical', not only in the teaching of writing but across many disciplinary and subject fields. Twenty years of writing research have brought great advances in our understanding of writing process, contexts for writing, and classroom strategies for fostering the individual writer's voice. But the role of the personal remains a dominant but poorly theorised and inadequately conceptualised notion. While an explosion of knowledges from critical discourse analysis and feminist poststructuralism provides new tools for analysis, writing pedagogies, for the most part, have not called upon critical understandings of language, text, discourse and subjectivity now available in the formulation of classroom practice.

In this book I bring together these diverse bodies of knowledge in order to relocate the personal within the social, cultural and political domains. My aim is to experiment with alternate, more theorised ways of reading and writing the personal. Working against the notion that meaning is ever simply personal, individual or private, I develop four teaching case studies in different educational sites (secondary, undergraduate, graduate, adult/community) to explore a montage of ways of working critically, rather than promote a single prescriptive answer. My approach is eclectic but not atheoretical, theorised but not abstract, demonstrating embodied ways of working critically with personal experience and text production.

Of course, the process of developing this pedagogy has itself been a journey of relocation, which I now map more specifically in the remainder of this chapter. My aim is to construct an autoethnography with the self-consciousness of a writing teacher. I need to decide which stories to include, how to sequence them, which to leave out. I wish to move in and out of the present to the future and past in order to represent my pedagogy of relocation as an amalgam—an intertextual borrowing of theories. Thus I locate myself as a situated subject in a mesh of discourses about language and text, including process pedagogies of the early 1980s, genre pedagogies of the mid 1980s, and critical discourse analysis and feminist poststructuralist work in the 1990s. I interweave my history as a teacher, student and researcher of writing with more general movements in the field in order to establish a critical perspective on writing and establish the ground for later chapters.

However, locations are never neutral, and Kirsch and Ritchie (1995) are right to remind us that it is not enough to locate ourselves in our scholarship and research—'to make the facile statements that often appear at the beginning of research articles' (1995:9), without also investigating what has shaped the writer's knowledge, including what is contradictory, unpleasant, unknowable. While it is important to claim the legitimacy of our experience, a 'politics of location' also demands a rigorously reflexive examination of ourselves as researchers and writers—and of our locations as 'fluid, multiple and illusive' (1995:8).

BEHIND THE CAMERA/OUT FROM UNDER THE TABLE: NEW HAMPSHIRE 1980

My academic career began in 1976 at a rural university in Australia—but it was my first sabbatical in 1980 at the University of New Hampshire that marks my obsession with writing research. Donald Graves hands me a video camera and suggests I use it to frame my observations in the New Hampshire elementary writing classrooms where he has invited me to observe. These are the last six months of his two-year National Institute of Education-funded study, where Graves and colleagues Susan Sowers and Lucy Calkins are documenting the writing behaviours of children in grades 1–4.

Graves' offer is generous. I am to locate myself in any classroom I like and focus on my own research questions during my four-month sabbatical in New Hampshire. I've read a number of Graves' research reports in *Language Arts* but have done no writing research myself and don't know what to expect. Giddy with freedom and terrified by stereotyped notions of research as disembodied, scientific work, I wonder what to look for and how I will know when I've found it. Such preoccupations may be peculiar to my middle–class good–girl desire–to–please. There are signs, however, that even in these early days of research, I understand 'look-ing' as a partial and political act; that the rooms where we locate ourselves and the directions in which we point our camera are never neutral decisions.

I notice, for example, that many of the research articles written by Graves and Calkins focus on the work of a par-ticular grade 1 teacher—who herself has begun to research her own classroom and run workshops for other teachers. I spend time in this teacher's room and am impressed with her facility in writing conferences. I am trying to see the pattern of her questions and how these scaffold children's subsequent drafts. But I am also uneasy. I am not attracted by stars. It may be that they have enough attention already, or it may be an act of rebellion. Coming from Australia, I am viewing with an outsider's obsession to understand how process writ-ing practices are put in place. This is 1980 and no one in Australia is interested yet. I relocate myself in a grade 2 classroom where I will subsequently document the cycle of publication of one child as she interacts with her skilful teacher in writing conferences (Kamler 1980).

Years later I come to understand that when we take cam-eras into classrooms we construct a set of positionings and relations of power for the 'human objects' we are viewing (see, for example, Reid *et al* 1996). A five-year-old writer named Zoe provides one lesson in 1983 when after being viewed by my camera for over a year, she asks if her friend Kate can join her during a writing interview scheduled at lunchtime. I agree but am surprised to hear her whisper on video, 'Kate, now you can be another famous writer in our class—just like me'. While Zoe's 'promise of Hollywood' is chastening, it is not until a decade later, when I research the construction of gendered subjectivities in the first month of school (Kamler *et al* 1994), that I more fully understand the partiality of the camera and its role in producing data.

In his discussion of ethnographic film, Nichols (1981) makes problematic the idea that a film transpar-ently discloses the real rather than producing through a set of discourses a particular reality. Facts

are not simply out there in the visible world; they
are themselves constituted. . . . The camera is one
of a range of sources of information about the event,
and it permits an extension of the number of readings that can be made. Its view and its record are
just as partial and as interested as those of the other
observers. (Reid *et al* 1996:100)

Of course, in 1980 my view of data was not framed, as it
is now, by feminist and poststructuralist theorising, and I
necessarily took a less critical view of data collection. It was
only gradually that I came to understand I was not simply
filming data which preexisted my entry to the research site—
that the data was not simply there waiting to be scooped up
by my camera. The camera itself is not a neutral tool of research. Looking, like writing, is a kind of composing—a selecting and ignoring—a looking and not-looking.

Writing about what I saw behind the camera in 1980,
however, was transforming. This writing was scaffolded by
Don Murray's graduate writing seminar at the University of
New Hampshire where I used my observations in the New
Hampshire primary classrooms as the focus of my major
research paper. I now see that seminar and my sabbatical
more broadly as a series of simultaneous, multiple relocations—a return to the United States after eight years in
Australia—a return with a three-year-old son, a collapsed
marriage behind me and tense negotiations with a family
ambivalent about my return because it was temporary.

Sabbaticals are times for reflection and writing—times
for intellectual work outside the teaching, administration,
committee work and political negotiations we call our daily
work. They are also times for renewal, and we are fortunate
to have them. Australian academics, however, are expected
to produce measurable outcomes from these times away—to
write books, papers, journal articles, research grant applications. While traces of the personal can be gleaned from book
acknowledgments which insiders read as voraciously as gos-
sip columns, academics rarely write *about* these times as a
space where we live our lives differently.

I am 33 years old. I am on sabbatical for six months living in a one-bedroom apartment with my three-year-old son. I am a single mother displaced—occupying a strange city without my usual child care networks—in order to work with Graves and Murray. The two Dons. It's a joke Australians understand differently because we have been shaped by the commercial jingle of the Don Smallgoods Manufacturer (Is Don, Is Good).

My task for Murray's seminar is to write a five-page paper each week for the next ten weeks. Fifty pages dredged up on ten topics of my choosing—as long as they pertain to the topic of writing. But I have a problem. I cannot write without cigarettes and I have just quit. After fifteen years as an addict, I threw my cigarettes away at my brother's home only three weeks earlier—trying to emulate him and my sister. In two years time, when our mother dies of lung cancer at age 58, I will be happy I too have quit, but I'm not happy now.

Now I'm unbalanced, deranged. I eat truckloads of food. I go to sleep at 8:00 P.M. with my son to make sure I don't smoke in the evening. I take hot baths at 3:00 A.M. when I'm awakened by nicotine desire. And when I am rock–bottom–ashtray–sucking–desperate, I inhale bits of marijuana to quell the tormenting red panic that rises in my chest and threatens to strangle me. The panic is not unfamiliar. I have quit before—three times in five years—and failed.

My failure each time is due to writing. It is writing which always brings me back. I vow to stop killing myself each summer and quit. I learn to talk on the phone, drink at parties, even finish a meal in a restaurant without nicotine. But then the new semester begins, the lectures, memos, journal articles, book chapters, faculty submissions pile up. I scavenge old ashtrays and sneak down the hall to 'borrow' a few from my colleague 'the smoker'. I light cigarettes so I won't flee the writing table. The cigarette in my hand makes the writing more tolerable, the staring into space less lonely. When I suck deeply the panic about having nothing to say eases. It's a physical sensation—the sweet–sucking–smoke calms me, gives me control—of the writing—my life. After one week I am back—a pack a day and the writing gets done.

But this time I am resolute. So I choose the topic of writing and smoking for my first seminar paper. It seems a banal topic but I can think of nothing else. My life is so constricted by my desire for cigarettes, there is nothing else.

As the seminar due date approaches I grow more out–of–control. I rehearse phrases before falling asleep, run fragments of ideas during the day. Anything but sit at the table and write. When finally I get there, it's worse than I expect. I pace, make gallons of tea and coffee, watch Sesame Street and Mr Rogers with my son, fantasise about meeting a tall, dark stranger who smokes. My head is pounding. I take aspirins and more hot baths. I sigh continuously but nothing eases my anxiety.

I read Murray's *Listening to Writing* (1982). 'Most craftsmen' [*sic*], Murray writes, 'are compulsive about their tools, and writers write with pen, pencil, typewriter and paper which is familiar to hand and eye'. It occurs to me that cigarettes have been my one and only tool for writing. And it may be that cigarettes have made it harder for me to write, not easier. It is true cigarettes increase my sense of control. They squash down the rising panic, which is why I love them. But lighting up keeps things from wandering into a mess and Murray argues that writing demands letting go, being surprised, writing junk. I am worried by this thought; it may be an addict's delusion or a sign I am on the road to reform.

In the end time runs out and I'm desperate to get something down. It may be that the critic in my head is also withdrawing from lack of nicotine. Of course, the irony is that this most unscholarly topic allows me to WRITE WITHOUT CIGARETTES for the first time. Ever. Five pages are filled and I do not die, although it is still a possibility. And when the paper

is finished all traces of my agony are removed—
except as I choose to tell it.

In the weeks ahead I will continue to hate writing but will find healthier writing obsessions. I will
spend hours in stationery shops searching for black
pilot razor point pens and green faintly-lined spiral-
bound notebooks. I will sing the praises of my green
velour beanbag lap-top desk and I will write everywhere—on my bed, outside while my son plays, on
trains and planes. I will pretend for the moment
that cigarettes don't write my papers. And that I
will never have to quit again.

Murray's valuable contribution to the field of composition is embodied in my experience of that seminar. We met
in the basement of Murray's house to read our papers out
loud for response and critique. The group liked my paper on
writing and smoking and I remember the moist orange pound
cake and sweet cinnamon buns baked by Minnie Mae Murray,
a woman who welcomed me to New Hampshire and gave me
her daughter's boots so I could tromp through New Hampshire snow with dry Australian feet.

I came to believe, as others before me, that Murray taught
me to write, even though his own pedagogy disavowed such
a claim. His notion of the writing conference created a
theorised space for gaining distance on writing and taught me
how to sit at the table with writers—hesitantly at first—and
ask questions about their writing. It created space for me to
move out from under my mother's kitchen table and find a
position from which to write with greater ease and confidence.

Conference questions—the form they take, when and why
and how to ask them—will become the focus of my evolving
writing pedagogy over the next twenty years. When conferencing is demeaned by advocates of genre-based pedagogy as a
laissez-faire, do-gooder progressive practice, I will resist—
but later struggle with what it means to make conference
questions more critical, so that they position writers to read
texts for traces of discourses. What is certain is that the
conference relocates the writer in relation to her writing—it

creates a seeing, hearing, embodied space or, in Soja's terms, a 'postmodern landscape . . . for revealing "other spaces" and hidden geographical texts' (1989:2).

DEEP IN THE PROCESS: AUSTRALIA 1980–84

There is some synergy in my timing. I am a young academic without a PhD, as is the tradition in Australian universities until the late 1980s. I return from New Hampshire ten pounds heavier, full of energy for classroom-based writing research and obsessed with my new electric typewriter. I am filled with the zeal of the newly converted. I am writing every day. I rise at 5:00 A.M. to make sure I write for at least two hours before my son rises.

Six months after my return to Australia, Graves comes to Sydney as an invited keynote speaker at the Third International English Teaching Conference in September 1980. It is difficult to recapture the excitement Graves generates in Australia (especially in the years since the critique of his work has been so well rehearsed), but his address is an historic moment which has a profound effect on writing pedagogy at all levels: elementary, secondary, university and adult education sectors.

The Primary English Teachers Association sponsors a book with Graves' address and papers by colleagues from the University of New Hampshire. The title, *Donald Graves in Australia: Children Want to Write* (Walsh 1981), highlights the Australian focus on the man (his talents for humour, metaphor, conversation) as much as his work. The inclusion of my chapter in the book (Kamler 1981) and Graves' reference to my New Hampshire research in his keynote address ensure that I begin to receive phone calls from all over Australia to do Graves workshops. I say I do Kamler—if they want that I'll come.

This is the time of the post–Whitlam funding boom when infrastructure and financial resources are available to induct teachers into progressive pedagogies. As I begin to develop writing workshops for teachers, I am committed to a teacher–

as–writer model but have to work around the limited time available to Australian teachers during their summer break. There can be no summer school like the Bay Area Writing Projects in California. Australian teachers get only six weeks vacation, not ten like their American colleagues, and they cannot spend half that time writing. They need recovery and family time. I remember. I have left the secondary classroom only four years earlier.

So a colleague and I develop a five-day intensive workshop structure. We establish a process writing paradigm using Murray's (1982) well-known 'index card' exercise to get started—Macrorie's (1980) 'telling facts' to develop detail in the writing and a 'tightening' exercise to teach editing skills. We structure group and individual conferences to ask questions of the writing, and on the final day we ask teachers to read their writing in the public arena as spoken publication. As each person reads the writing they have developed during the week, the tension is high, the atmosphere animated. No one knows how this will go. The first time it is exhilarating—and the time after that—and the time after that. The writing is tight and sharp, it is focused and works on different levels; the weaknesses are glossed and carried by the energy of the spoken voice that reads the text into being.

While the writing is powerful and seems to make a difference to people's lives, I have no way to theorise the effect. The process paradigm in which I'm located does not help me. There are, however, some scenes which disturb me and which I write off to the unpredictable power of writing.

> It is 4:00 P.M. We are at a five-day residential workshop in a country town called Bendigo (160 km) outside of Melbourne—with wide leafy streets and a stunning cathedral. We are working/living in a motel complex. We have just completed the second day, and participants have been in their rooms writing during the afternoon. There's a knock at my door. A woman enters. She is in her early 40s, her hair slightly dishevelled and backlit as she stands in the doorway. She will not sit down. 'You've ru-

ined my life, you know, you've ruined it. I had no
intention of leaving my husband until the children
got older. But now I can't stay. You've ruined it'.

It is a chilling moment I cannot erase. Earlier that morning
the woman detailed in writing a scene at her dinner table.
She had been directed by me to identify a generalised statement in her draft ('they didn't communicate') and create a
'once' in Macrorie's (1980) sense—to locate a specific scene
that would exemplify the lack of communication she was
referring to. I asked her a number of questions about the
dinner party—the preparation, the menu, the guests, the
conversation. There was nothing in her answers that signalled danger to me, and she continued writing most of the
afternoon. As her teacher I found the act of transforming
her life scene into text, identifying the details and recreating the scene, energising.

However, the act of visualising tipped this woman over
and she blamed me. Although empathetic, I numbed myself
to her accusation and psychologised her. She was in pain,
transferring her hostility onto me. The part of me that felt
devastated and responsible, pushed these feelings away. I was
amazed at the force of her feelings, but I couldn't see my
complicity in building these meanings as I had no discourses
available to me other than psychology.

In building this critique of my practice, I do not wish to
disavow the value of this exercise retrospectively, or negate
the importance of working with the embodied specificity of
place and persons to create a spatialised text. What I do
wish to highlight is my own innocence and naïveté with
regard to the strategy. There were students other than Nadia
who became upset over the years, who cried or became
aggressive when the writing revealed discomforting insights.
I understood that detailing their experience in writing made
'real' the pain they lived with and that their aggression
towards me was misplaced or transferred, much as occurs
in therapy. I was not frightened by their emotion but certainly did not see myself as implicated. I will need other

discourses, such as Lee's (1997b) notion of coproduction to help me read such pedagogical moments from a different position.

THE GENRE YEARS, OR A STUDENT ONCE AGAIN: AUSTRALIA 1984–90

I am sitting in my PhD supervisor's office. We are bound in ways that may or may not happen in the United States where students are mentored by committees rather than single individuals. The dependency and intensity of the one-to-one relationship most Australian PhD students experience is complex but will not come under critical public scrutiny until postgraduate pedagogy begins to emerge as a significant area of scholarship and research in the mid-1990s (see, for example, Lee and Green 1996; Kamler and Threadgold 1996; Lee and Williams 1998).

I have travelled an hour and a half to meet with my supervisor. We are to focus on my transitivity analysis of five-year-old Zoe's texts. In Halliday's (1985) systemic functional grammar, six different types of transitivity processes are recognised in the language: material and behavioural (processes of doing), mental (processes of feeling and thinking), verbal (processes of saying), relational and existential (processes of being).

These differentiations of meaning are a great advance on traditional grammar descriptions of a verb as a 'doing' word. But the challenge of categorising more precisely the kind of meaning being made by the verb is not straightforward. Meaning is slippery and no matter how hard I try, I cannot pin down some of the processes in Zoe's text. I do not yet understand this as a problem of semantic grammars more generally. I am unaware, in fact, that it is this indeterminacy of meaning that makes the systemic functional grammar open to criticism in international linguistic circles. All I know, lowly PhD student that I am, is that my head aches from the effort of making such fine gradations of meaning. I feel stupid.

The process I have been struggling with is *had* as in *I had my party* and *I had my cake*. According to the bible (our affectionate term for Halliday's 387-page tome modestly titled *An Introduction to Functional Grammar* (1985) *had* is a relational process. There are three broad types of relational processes—intensive, circumstantial and possessive—which express different ways of being and are found in two modes—attributive and identifying. Halliday's example *Peter has a piano* is analysed as a relational/possessive process because the relationship between the two terms *Peter* and the *piano* is one of ownership, as in *Peter owns the piano*.

But this does not help me. Halliday does not analyse young children's writing, and I have the sense that *had* is being used in Zoe's text as a material process of doing, rather than one of owning. I have struggled with these two clauses and others like them for weeks, and depending on the time of day, my mood, the weather, I sometimes decide they are relational and sometimes material. Back and forth. I need an answer. I need to quantify the transitivity choices in Zoe's ten texts and look for patterns. I need to pin these processes down so I can move on.

I come to PhD work relatively late in my academic career, after working for eight years as a university teacher/writer/researcher. This is not unusual in Australian universities, particularly education faculties, where mid-career development has been the norm rather than the exception. Australian postgraduate work is a hybrid, which until recent years has owed more to British than American models. In the British tradition, great value is placed on completing an undergraduate degree and obtaining first-class honours. The British Master's is a no-coursework research-only degree, making it highly regarded as an entry qualification for researchers. As a consequence, many older eminent scholars in Britain and Australia do not have PhDs.

However, while it was once common for non-PhDs to obtain positions in Australian universities, this is no longer the case as credentialling requirements are shaped by global marketisation forces to more closely approximate those of the United States. Most of my colleagues in faculties of education around Australia do not enrol in PhD programs until at least 35 years of age, *after* they are employed in universities. This repositioning of oneself as student after years of being authorised as an 'expert' in one's field, constructs a different set of power relations than those faced by younger students without years of professional practice.

In order to make dissertation work possible, Australian academics engage in a variety of relocations. Some are granted extended leave to study in the United States where they remain until they complete their degrees; others return to Australia after completing coursework only and struggle to write their dissertations while recommencing full-time work. Some opt to study in Australian universities part-time—often where they are not employed—and rely on squeezing their writing time into evenings, weekends and occasional intense periods of three- to six-month leaves scattered over five to six years. A few of the privileged (to the extent that one can call quitting a full-time job and living on $12,000 a year a privilege) study full-time, often supported by Australian Commonwealth scholarships for up to a maximum of three years.

In 1984, I enrol as a part-time student while I continue full-time employment as a lecturer in language and literacy at a university 450 km away—a strange encounter of a third kind. The data I have been collecting for the past four years has come from process writing classrooms where I have been observing the youngest writers at school. Given the intense demand for professional development in the early 1980s, I have resisted the elision of Graves/process/'America knows best' by collecting early writing data from Australian classrooms and writing about it for conferences and publication.

When it comes to analysing children's writing, however, I have come up against a number of limitations of the process paradigm. In a chapter entitled "Observations of One Child Learning to Write in Two Classroom Contexts" (Kamler 1987), I focus on the relationship between five-year-old Peter's drawing and writing, the length of his texts, his control of spelling and handwriting and his self-concept as writer, but I have no tools for analysing the meaning of his texts or the text/context interface. I believe I need a principled way to analyse the text—to scrutinise not only *how* children have written but *what* they have written about.

So I come to systemic functional linguistics (Halliday 1985) and the work of genre theorists (Christie 1984, 1986; Kress 1985; Martin 1984; Rothery 1985) looking for new analytic tools to help me deconstruct children's writing. But I come as an innocent, unprepared for the battle I subsequently find myself embroiled in. In the years between my enrolment in 1984 and my graduation in 1990, Australian literacy educators engage in what has been called the genre-process debate (Reid 1987)—a sanitised term for what was often a volatile and bloody 'struggle over the agenda for literacy education in our schools and teacher education programs' (Green 1987:84). While genre advocates pushed for 'genre-consciousness', response on the process side ranged 'from moral outrage to polite but very firm refusal' (Green 1987:84).

Richardson (1991) and Threadgold (1988) provide a useful overview and critique of the various positions in that 'debate'. The 'forthright and unbending' nature (Richardson 1991:174) nature of the critique offered by genre advocates is captured in Martin's own outline of his position:

> With its stress on ownership and voice, its preoccupation with children selecting their own topics, its reluctance to intervene positively and constructively during conferencing, and its complete mystification of what has to be learned for children to produce effective written products, it is currently promoting a situation in which only the brightest middle–class children can possibly learn what is needed. Conferencing is used not to teach but to obscure. This kind of refusal to teach helps reinforce the success of ruling-class children in education; through an insidious benevolence other children are supportively encouraged to fail. (Martin 1985:61)

The question of where to position myself in this debate was vexed. The 'genre position' argued for more explicit teaching of linguistic and textual features, a more active role for the teacher and greater attention to factual as well as personal genres. These were critiques I supported. What I abhorred was the ahistorical refusal to acknowledge any benefits of process pedagogy. As Richardson argues:

> In establishing themselves in the academic, political and educational market places, the advocates of genre have been less than generous in recognising the achievements of the process/whole language group. Fifteen years ago we gave no consideration to "drafting," "revising," and "conferencing," they are now commonplace and teachers have a much better understanding of the complexity of learning to write and of teaching writing. (1991:185)

The genrist predilection for an oppositional politics seemed to promote careers and educational agendas more than it benefited teachers and students. The fact that this was a deliberate strategy to counter the hegemony of process approaches and to carve out a space for alternate critical work was later made explicit by Martin himself in an informal address to an Institute on Educational Research at the Australian Reading Association Conference in Adelaide in 1991.

It seems to me now, as it did then, that the way we argue our positions about writing pedagogy is as significant as the critique we make. Oppositional thinking is ahistorical—it reduces the complexities of pedagogy and oversimplifies differences between positions. It constructs a politics of 'correctness'; where one side must be seen as right and true, the other as wrong or outdated or theoretically and ideologically suspect. Bill Green (1987) argues that a failure to acknowledge history in curriculum debates is both dangerous and wasteful:

> It shouldn't really be necessary to make the point, but all too often is, that history matters, 'our' his-

tory, and we ignore or forget it only at our peril and always to our disadvantage.... The point is a very simple one. We have made significant advances in writing pedagogy over the past two decades. It is emphatically not the case of having to start from scratch. (1987:84)

As a doctoral student in 1986, however, it was difficult to find a speaking position outside the binary opposition of process and genre. I could not take up the evangelistic fervour of either process *or* genre; nor could I disavow process as an advance on traditional skill-based approaches or genre as an advance on process-based approaches. Frustrated by the impossibility of part-time study, I quit my job in 1988, withdrew from professional forums and enrolled as a full-time student. It would take years, however, until a developing critique of genre work emerged from a number of theoretical positions (eg, Luke 1994; Lee 1993; Poynton 1993; Kress and Threadgold 1988) and offered other discourses to critique the 'debate' itself (Kamler 1994, 1995a) and to relocate myself.

But at that moment in my supervisor's office, my concerns are different. I am struggling to analyse the transitivity in Zoe's texts and am amazed when my supervisor vacillates as I do between material and relational processes. I am also pleased as her uncertainty validates my own. When, however, she phones Halliday about these clauses—'I had my party' and 'I had my cake'—I am even more pleased as I know I will get an answer, at last. It is decided that the process is *both* material and possessive relational. And once the answer is given, that's what we call it. In my dissertation, I analyse the clauses as follows:

I	had	my party
Actor	*Process: material*	*Goal*

I	had	my cake
Carrier: possessor	*Process: relational possession*	*attribute: possessed*

It is an interesting feature of this orientation that the process *had* is classified as both a material process and a possessive process. Although we tend to think of young children's writing as simple, it often makes use of high-frequency items used in the language such as *had* which can be categorised in a number of different ways, depending on the kind of meaning they are making.

The first instance of *had* in the opening clause is classified as a material process. This is because *had* carries a sense of action rather than ownership. Having a party is an action in which invited guests participate, rather than an object which can be owned. Accordingly, it has been classified as a material process. In the second clause, by contrast, *had* has been classified as a possessive process. This is because it signifies ownership, whereby the cake is established as the principal participant of the text and Zoe as the owner of the cake. There is no sense in which the process signifies the action of eating, as in *I ate my cake*. Rather, it signifies owning the cake, which is the special privilege of the birthday girl. (Kamler 1990:411–12)

While this PhD text speaks authoritatively, the process of writing it inscribes in my body the certain knowledge that my own linguistic judgments are not to be trusted, that there is always a higher authority which needs to be consulted for verification. I do not realise at the time that it will take years to move beyond this sense of delegitimation. In later years I am grateful to Alison Lee (1996, 1997a) for her incisive critique of many of the systemic practices that positioned me, as a child, as without authority. In her discussion of the problems of what she calls a 'pedagogy of induction and mastery', she writes:

If, in the case of the successful outcome of a pedagogy of mastery, a student subject is 'properly' constructed as the 'good subject' of a discourse, in what sense might that subject be envisaged moving outside that framing to take up another position within an alternative, resisting or competing discourse? In other words, how can a student's 'own ends' be conceived outside the obedient and docile subject position, required for and achieved through apprenticeship? At the very least, this issue requires careful and sustained inquiry. (Lee 1997a:420–1)

It is discomforting to realise at the end of six years' work on a thesis entitled *Gender and Genre: A Case Study of a Girl and Boy Learning to Write* (Kamler 1990) that systemic linguistic theory helps me say little about gender and power relations in schooling. What the systemic analytic does allow is a rich description of the invisible ways gender is constructed by Zoe and Peter at all levels of text—both within the schematic structure and at finer levels of delicacy within the clause. But ultimately, I find linguistics an insufficient theoretical and methodological base from which to derive an analysis of literacy and gender.

Ahead lie a new set of theoretical relocations in poststructural feminist theorising and the loss of yet another innocent belief—that PhD work will finally give me the tools I require to do my academic work.

A TEACHER AGAIN:
POST–PHD PEDAGOGICAL CRISES 1991–1993

In 1991 I return to the academy as a newly credentialled university teacher. But between 1991 and 1993 I have two experiences that force me to abandon aspects of both writing process and genre pedagogies. Although separated in chronological time, these moments come together in memory as discursive moments of post–PhD crisis. PhD under arm, ready to relocate again in a new university politics, this Barbara is blissfully unaware that her subjectivity has been rewritten by the process of doing a PhD and that six years immersion in Halliday's theory of language as social semiotic (Halliday 1978, 1985)—where language is seen 'as a mode of

representation which constructs social realities, social identities and social relations as well as being constructed by
them' (Threadgold 1997:91)—will make it impossible for her
to simply return to her established teaching practices.

While the stories told so far suggest why she might refuse
an oppositional stance between process and genre, these cri-
ses in teaching work somewhat differently, as critical moments when her collusion as coproducer of unexamined
gendered meanings is too visible to ignore—when she is forced
to attend more critically to the ways she encourages students
to tell their stories and to her part in shaping the texts students produce. These moments can be framed as two separate cautionary tales of lost innocence.

TILL DEATH DO US PART

The first tale tells the story of a university teacher interacting with a 19-year-old education student about her writing.
The setting is a writing workshop where the teacher has
asked students to draft, revise and conference a text of personal experience over a period of four weekly meetings. The
topic is a personal experience of the student's choosing. While
the text itself is ungraded, students are asked to use it to reflect
on the process of writing in workshop settings and imagine
possible applications for their future work as teachers.

The teacher's commitment to teaching writing and revision
strategies in the university is not new. In Australian universities, there is an absence of composition—not because of the
historically low status of composition in the English curriculum (Miller 1990; Clifford and Schlib 1994), but because there
is no compulsory historical space where students are asked to
focus on their own writing. As an American, the teacher finds
this amazing and over the years has searched for ways to build
space into her literacy subjects for teaching writing.

Australian universities have devised a variety of structures
to fill this vacuum, the most common being the development
of tertiary writing skills units, located outside the academic
disciplines, as an academic support to students (with all the
attendant difficulties facing a mostly female, untenured

workforce). In the best contexts, the literacy expert (a nonaca-demic) collaborates with a subject specialist (an academic) in a coordinated and respectful manner to help students learn to write the university in discipline-specific ways (Bartholomae 1985; see Golebiowski and Borland 1997 for a comprehensive view of tertiary literacy practices in Australian universities).

This teacher believes the best way to teach education students how to teach writing is to ask them to write them-selves. When she returns to teaching post-PhD, she therefore builds in a four-week workshop cycle of drafting, conferencing and workshopping, culminating in the production of a pub-lishable text. But all does not go well for a second-year edu-cation student named Amy.

Amy has written a draft about her upcoming marriage at the end of the semester to a man who works at the Ford factory. Her text is full of generalisation and cliché, and in a writing conference her teacher attempts to locate the specific details behind her generalisations: Where was she? What was her partner doing, wearing? What was she doing, feeling and thinking? The young woman is resistant to her teacher's ques-tions, but the teacher persists, believing Amy will see the point once the details begin to emerge in her text.

Two weeks later, on the final day of the workshop, Amy reads 'Till Death Do Us Part' to the group. Her text begins with an egalitarian preamble detailing the importance of men and women being equal partners in marriage, sharing house-hold responsibilities and working together to sustain romance and respect. In subsequent paragraphs, Amy details a scene which occurs twice a week when she and John, her future husband, spend the evening together.

In her text John is sprawled on the sofa drinking beer after an exhausting day at the Ford factory, while she, also weary from a full day at university, works in the kitchen to prepare their dinner. Amy explains with certainty that al-though she and John will share the cooking after marriage, she most often prepares dinner on these weekly visits be-cause John is so tired. Dinner is a time-consuming leg of lamb and three vegetables—which Amy serves on trays while she and John watch The Dating Game on TV—happy they do not have to suffer the public indignity of finding a mate in front of millions of viewers, because they have one another.

As Amy reads her text, her teacher searches the room for other distressed faces but finds only one—an older student whose raised eyebrows signal her amazement at contradictions no one else in the room seems to hear. In that moment, the teacher realises her questioning of Amy in conference has indeed helped Amy construct a more detailed text, but one that now constructs gender and class as unproblematic and inscribes patriarchal discourses as natural.

Because the teacher's workshop practices celebrated the writer's personal voice, it is impossible for her to discuss the contradiction between Amy's egalitarian preamble, for example, and the domestic scene she details in her text. Such a discussion could only be read by Amy as personal criticism—as a critique of her life, hopes and dreams. The personalist discourses which dominate the writing workshop enforce the teacher's silence, as she realises in horror her own collusion in helping Amy inscribe—in detail—a gendered fiction presented as truth—complete with cultural icons of beer, television, apron and stove. The teacher finds only one certainty in that moment—that she must stop teaching personal writing in such workshops. Until she can find a way to reframe personal writing so that it is not simply confessional, not simply elided with the self, she must stop. And she does. For four years.

A number of recent studies have documented similar problems in elementary and secondary classrooms, showing that writing workshops are never simply benign places where students work harmoniously with teachers to celebrate the writer's personal voice. In the United States, writers such as Delpit (1988), Dyson (1992), Dressman (1993) and Lensmire (1994, 1998) have shown that despite ostensible benefits of process workshop approaches, they disadvantage lower income and minority student populations in terms of gender, class and race. In Australia, studies by Kamler (1993) and Gilbert (1993a) have demonstrated that texts produced in elementary process writing classrooms construct a gendered representation of personal experience and masculinist discourses of violence. Australian genre theorists such as Martin (1991) and Christie

(1990) have critiqued process writing notions of personal ownership and personal voice and argued that a wide variety of
genres need to be taught, including explicit knowledge of the
linguistic and textual features of those genres, if students are
to be empowered as powerful members of their culture.

Genre theorists also posited a genre pedagogy as a corrective to these ideological deficiencies of process. On grounds
of equity and empowerment, they argued that a less personalist, more explicit pedagogy would benefit those groups disenfranchised by Australian society. However, my second tale,
'Girls into Concrete', suggests such claims may be blind to
their own masculinst and patriarchal assumptions.

GIRLS INTO CONCRETE

This tale of lost innocence tells of the same university teacher
interacting, this time, with an off-campus student, a practising teacher who has enrolled in a graduate diploma in language and literacy in order to upgrade her qualification. The
setting is a course on children's writing, located within a
systemic linguistic theoretical framework and genre-based
approaches to teaching writing (Christie 1989). As part of
their assignment, students are to select a genre, teach it within
a curriculum context of their choosing and closely analyse
the texts of six students, using the systemic analytic. Based
on the success with which children construct the genre, students are to evaluate the success or otherwise of their lessons and make recommendations for improvement.

The teacher's commitment to the systemic functional
grammar is a legacy of her PhD, although she finds Halliday's
(1985) work on grammatical structure—on clauses and how
they are structured to mean—to be far more useful than the
genre-based pedagogy which uses understandings of this grammar. The technical complexity of mastering the systemic
linguistic analytic, however, is great; the years of apprenticeship many. The question of how much linguistics teachers
need—taught when, how and for what purposes—will plague
her for years to come. (Chapters 3 and 5 demonstrate some of
the ways this dilemma has been resolved). At this point in

time, however, the teacher believes an explicit understanding of text structure, of the relation between text and context, and of the differences between spoken and written language can help her students become more able teachers of writing.

The text called 'Girls into Concrete' was produced in a grade three classroom and submitted by a graduate diploma student named Carolyn.

GIRLS INTO CONCRETE

This potion will turn girls into concrete

INGREDIANCE

1 kg of concrete
2 girls
1 eye from a bat

METHOD

1. tip 1 kg of concrete into tub
2. drop eye into concrete in tub
3. put girls into concrete. make sure that girls are sitting up right

NOTE

This potion will not work if you add too much concrete

As requested, Carolyn analysed the linguistic features of this text to demonstrate that her grade 3 writer, John, had indeed created an instance of a procedural genre. Her detailed analysis, abbreviated here, highlights Carolyn's discussion of the following characteristics of the genre:

- transitivity processes are almost exclusively material to build the sequence of actions required to make the brew;
- material processes are in the imperative mood (tip, drop, put) and are all in Theme position, so the action/command serves to carry the text forward to direct the reader;

- reference is at all times generic rather than specific (referring to all girls, for example, rather than specific girls);
- a sense of sequence is made explicit by use of numbers in the method;
- the tenor is authoritative and impersonal, and the writer's identity does not intrude into the text as is common in genres of personal experience, such as Recount or Observation.

Carolyn's analysis is competent in its own terms; it reproduces a number of linguistic and generic features which are characteristic of systemic analyses of text, as these are set out for teachers in a variety of genre-based materials (see, for example, Disadvantaged Schools Program 1988; Christie 1989; Christie *et al.* 1990; Derewianka 1990). What is shocking to her teacher, however, are the absences in her discussion—the fact that she makes no comment about the gendered meanings in John's text. There is no analysis of the misogynist violence being done to girls' bodies or of the male writer's construction of female as victim. The imperatives certainly do build authority in the text, but they do so by directing the reader to immobilise the girl's body and turn her into a stationary object. The act of making female-object is made literal in the text in the pouring of concrete, a material process, indeed, but one which presumably causes the death of the subject through this concretisation.

Not only does Carolyn fail to see such meanings or comment on them as significant, but she colludes in the construction herself by making the following suggestion at the end of her analysis:

> While I would classify text 2 as a complete instructional procedural genre, it would have been even better with a concluding step after step 3 of the method—eg, 4. When concrete girls have set can be used as ornaments in home or garden.

Her remark demonstrates the extent to which she has been positioned by the terms of the pedagogy she enacts. In striving to make the generic structure more complete, Carolyn presents her suggestion as neutral and unproblematic. Her teacher, however, is highly distressed and again sees her collusion in producing this text. When she phones Carolyn to ask permission to use the text and raise her concerns, Carolyn suggests she is overreacting, that the writer John is just having a bit of fun and that this kind of thing goes on all the time in primary school.

Exactly the point. The construction of gender is such a dominating set of social practices in schools that mysogynist meanings are naturalised and unseen, or seen and minimised because boys will be boys and after all they are only children. This ignores the fact, highlighted by Walkerdine (1990) and other theorists operating from feminist and poststructuralist positions, that boys can take the position of men through language; they can gain material power by constituting girls in text (even cementing them in) as powerless objects of sexist discourses.

The intention here is not to highlight Carolyn's inadequacies as a teacher or analyst. Her response is not unique, nor is her work a poor instance of the pedagogy she was asked to implement. It is to highlight her teacher's crisis of understanding that the genre pedagogy and systemic analytic constitute a powerful technology which prevent Carolyn from reading the gendered meanings in John's text. Because her own PhD used systemics to make gendered meanings visible, the teacher assumed these tools were potentially emancipatory.

Clearly, however, Carolyn's reading of the text is dependent on the way in which she is positioned in relation to it (Kress 1985). The practices of the instructional genre are difficult for her to identify because she is so firmly fixed on specifying textual characteristics and linguistic features (as her teacher requested). What is overlooked, in the process, are the networks of power that are sustained and brought into existence by the text and the ways these contribute to and reproduce social injustices (Gilbert 1993b). In order to produce a more critical reading, Carolyn needs access to other discourses, rather than more sophisticated understandings of the systemic analytic.

In short, she cannot foreground the gendered nature of the generic conventions because the linguistic tools are not sufficient to examine the relations of power operating. In the months and years that follow, her teacher will come to understand, following Lee (1993), that linguistics is an insufficient theoretical and methodological base from which to derive a pedagogy of writing. 'What is missing is, among other things, a social theory of discourse which acknowledges simultaneously the complexity and materiality of the negotiation of power relations in social practices' (1993:132).

As our teacher holds up the two texts, 'Till Death Do Us Part', in one hand, 'Girls into Concrete' in the other, she resists the temptation to throw both in the bin and erase her complicity in their production. Instead, she tucks them under her pillow—a reminder that unexamined gendered meanings will be made and remade in writing, regardless of which pedagogy is put in place, unless teachers have a theoretical frame to make such meanings visible. She dismisses the easy assumption that a genre pedagogy constitutes a critical literacy or that process approaches should be abandoned because they essentialise the personal. She wants ultimately to argue for a different way of thinking about writing the personal, to open up new spaces that cannot simplistically be labelled either process or genre.

MAPPING THE LANDSCAPE

The chapters which follow chart her struggle to theorise a new set of writing practices—a critical writing pedagogy— that relocates the personal through her engagement with feminist and poststructural theorising. Each chapter highlights a different aspect of the work, none complete in itself nor presenting itself as a new writing orthodoxy. The focus throughout is on experimentation and innovation—on positioning student writers as coresearchers who produce stories and subject these to a critical process of analysis and theorising.

Chapter 2 retheorises notions of voice and transformation as these have been used in a variety of critical and emancipatory pedagogies. Ultimately, I reject *voice* as a conceptual framework for writing and opt instead for a construct of narrative because it allows a closer attention to textuality and representation. I argue as well for a more modest, semiotic notion of transformation where writing is conceptualised as a space for transforming both the text and the writer's subjectivity.

Chapters 3 to 6 delineate what a critical writing pedagogy might look like in particular secondary, undergraduate, postgraduate and adult education sites. The specificity of these portraits allows me to explore what is an appropriate pedagogy for different purposes, differently located subjects and different institutional contexts.

Chapter 3 focuses on the 'stories of ageing' workshops where women aged 60 to 90 wrote stories which challenge the narrow range of negative images of ageing that are pervasive in our culture. Chapter 4 examines a 16-year-old high school student struggling to write argument and adopt the subjectivity required to assert authority in text. Chapter 5 examines undergraduate teacher education students learning to use critical discourse analysis to analyse their own writing and that of their high school students. Chapter 6 presents cultural biographies written for a Master's course on language, gender and education and examines students' reflections on the effects of this writing on their lives. Chapter 7 identifies key features of a critical writing pedagogy that can be gleaned from these specific, disciplinary contexts—a pedagogy that aims to foster agency and social action in the politics of particular writing classrooms.

CHAPTER TWO

Relocating Voice and Transformation

❖

The history I have told in chapter 1 locates my interest in the personal—in the critical—in relocation—in embodied ways that foreground my lived experience as student, teacher, researcher, daughter, mother. I have shown how the pedagogy I call critical occurs at the intersection of both process and genre pedagogies without valorising or simply rejecting either. My critique has been written as a juxtaposition of embodied spaces, following Brodkey's premise that

> space is as crucial a component of critical theory as time because cartography, like history, is the prerogative of the powerful and the representation of space a discursive means of naturalizing and rationalizing the inequities of the present.
>
> Specifically, cartography designates certain spaces as sites. As I am using it here, a site is a space whose definition is critical to maintaining hegemony *and* to countering it. (1996a:177)

In chapter 2 I continue the project of locating and relocating—but differently, by more directly addressing the sites of scholarship that inform the critical writing pedagogy I propose. In particular, I address two conceptual fields that need to be relocated in a discussion of the personal: voice and transformation.

Voice is a recurring metaphor in writing process (alternately referred to as writing workshop) pedagogies where 'students are advised to find their own voices in writing, teachers are advised to listen to such voices, and a clear personal voice in writing is often regarded as the mark of an effective writer' (Gilbert 1990:61). Voice also plays a central role in a variety of critical, democratic and emancipatory pedagogies where it has been used as a motivation to write, as a mode of politicisation, as a way to understand and disrupt patriarchy and other oppressive formations.

I will argue in this chapter for a notion of voice that is situated—not singular but multiple—a notion that calls on both writing workshop and critical pedagogies but which is relocated by feminist and poststructural theorising. To argue for a notion of situated voice is to invoke the geographical and spatial metaphors that organise this book. It is to argue for a voice that is always located—always related to a particular context—and to reject a universal call for the voice that will simply empower she who writes. Ultimately, my aim is to argue for a notion of the personal which is not simply equated with voice.

With regard to transformation, I argue that writing the personal has power to transform both the writer's subjectivity and the text produced. I locate my argument, however, outside extravagant claims and discourses of writing as 'therapy' or 'empowerment,' where the writer's voice is seen to be the mechanism for changing the person and the world—for the attainment of universal, abstract goals of liberation and social transformation.

Instead, I argue for a notion of transformation that is more modest, more semiotic, more textual—and for a critical pedagogy that creates distance, a theorised space to analyse texts of personal experience as discursively produced and therefore changeable.

RELOCATING VOICE

In the following discussion I examine how voice has been conceptualised in a variety of discourses. Spatially, I move across a number of educational sites (elementary, secondary, university), disciplinary sites (writing process, critical, feminist, teacher education, composition, curriculum studies) and continents (Australia, North America, Europe) in ways that may disturb those who hold to more boundaried practices of theorising their discursive fields.

In the Australian context in which I teach, however, we are a smaller community of scholars who of necessity talk and conference across boundaries. We do not, for example, have separate conferences on college composition, language arts and secondary English education, and we must, by virtue of our geographical isolation, make it our business to know more about North American, British and Canadian theorising than they know about us. We regularly travel to international conferences, relocate our lives overseas during sabbatical more frequently than our colleagues come to Australia, although this has altered somewhat in recent years with increased interest in Australian-based critical literacy (eg, Muspratt *et al.* 1997) and the Australian editorship of such journals as the *Journal of Adolescent and Adult Literacy* and *Discourse*.

Tim Lensmire's (1998) critique and reconception of voice are particularly relevant to my concerns here as he speculates about what voice means not just for an emancipatory educational politics but for the actual writing practices enacted in (mostly elementary) classrooms. Lensmire draws an extended comparison between two conceptions of voice: the first he calls *voice as individual expression* which is promoted by advocates of writing workshop approaches such as Calkins (1986), Graves (1983), Murray (1985) and Atwell (1987), who call for students to express their unique selves in writing; the second, *voice as participation* is elaborated by advocates of critical pedagogy including Freire (1970, 1985), Simon (1987), Giroux (1988), and Giroux and McLaren (1989) who call for critical dialogues among students and teachers as a mode of empowerment.

Lensmire outlines the serious problems with both conceptions and proposes an alternative—where voice is conceived of as a 'project involving appropriation, social struggle and becoming' (1998:262). Importantly, he acknowledges the history of the pedagogies he would critique—without simply creating a 'yes, but . . . ' genre. He highlights two important aspects of the writing workshop emphasis on voice: (1) its commitment to 'taking students' experiences and meanings seriously, in contrast to traditional pedagogies that often run roughshod over personal meaning in the name of teacher control and convention' (1998:266), and (2) its commitment to a pedagogy of engagement, which gives students agency to actively pursue topics they find compelling and meaningful.

He highlights as well the dangers of an apolitical imperative to 'find your own voice', 'a voice that expresses who you are' (1998:263), particularly when that same voice is either celebrated uncritically or monitored in classrooms to eradicate difference. The idea that there is a real authentic self that can be expressed in writing is, at best, a partial notion grounded in an Enlightenment conception 'in which the self is imagined to be stable, coherent, unitary and autonomous' (1998:264).

Lensmire argues, like many poststructural feminist scholars, that to assume a stable preexistent self that can be expressed in writing is to assume that language itself is simply a tool for that expression, a neutral vehicle for making and expressing preexistent meaning—rather than a site of struggle where subjectivity and meaning are produced. It is to ignore that the act of writing does not simply express a self, but has serious effects on the self that is writing. It is to ignore, further, that writers are not isolated individuals pursuing personal meaning but are embedded in social relations of gender, race, class and sexuality that influence the work of writing and creating a self.

Voice as participation (a conception promoted by critical pedagogy), by contrast, is characterised by Lensmire as a less romantic, more politicised conception, grounded in issues of power, difference and struggle. Rather than voice signalling the unique expression of a unitary unfettered self, the self envisaged by critical pedagogy is multiple and social, created out of the cultural resources at hand, including experiences, languages, histories, stories. Student voice is central to the emancipatory educational project of empowering students, 'in the name of social justice, equality and democratic community; and in preparation for and as part of transformative social action' (1998:267).

Within such a pedagogy, voice is the starting point, the basis for the collective work to be done. Student writing about the self is valued because it affirms the student's own language and experience and because it provides texts for the classroom community to examine, critique and learn from. Because critical pedagogy locates student voice in a social self that is shaped within an oppressive society that privileges certain meanings, it advocates a critical interrogation of voice—where student writing is not only affirmed, but questioned. Within workshop pedagogy, by contrast, voice is the goal—the desired endpoint for any given piece of student writing—the criteria by which its success is measured.

While Lensmire's preference is for the more politicised version of voice theorised by critical pedagogy, he also critiques its failure to embed student voice in the immediate local contexts of the classroom—and to engage with what the conflict of voices (between students, students and teachers and within the individual student) means for the production of writing in the classroom.

This is a point elaborated by a number of poststructural feminist scholars who take a far more critical position on the notion of voice advocated by critical pedagogy than Lensmire. Elizabeth Ellsworth (1992), drawing on her attempts to practice antiracist pedagogy in the university classroom, critiques voice as a dehistoricised, abstract notion that does not engage with a politics of difference. While critical pedagogy shares some of the assumptions of those working from antiracist and poststructuralist feminist positions—that 'any individual woman's politicized voice will be partial, multiple, and contradictory' (1992:103)—Ellsworth argues that:

it does not confront the ways in which any individual student's voice is already a 'teethgritting' and
often contradictory intersection of voices constituted
by gender, race, class, ability, ethnicity, sexual orientation, or ideology. Nor does it engage with the
fact that the particularities of historical context,
personal biography, and subjectivities . . . render each
expression of student voice partial and predicated
on the absence and marginalization of alternative
voices. (1992:103–4)

The need to productively acknowledge and work with
difference is central to Mimi Orner's (1992) critique of voice.
Orner argues that '[s]tudent voice, as it has been conceptual-
ized in work which claims to empower students, is an oppressive construct—one that . . . perpetuates relations of
domination in the name of liberation' (1992:75). 'When Anglo-
American feminist and critical pedagogues call for students
to find and articulate their voice, they . . . deny their own
subjectivity, their own positionality, the partiality of their
own voices' (1992:86). They see themselves as empowered to
help students value their own language and background but
never imagine that their own modes of relating need to be
scrutinised or that they may also 'contribute to the racism,
ethnocentrism, classism, sexism, heterosexism and so on that
their students experience' (1992:87).

Orner, like Ellsworth, suggests it is naive to think there
can be anything like a genuine sharing of voices in the classroom. 'What does seem possible . . . is an attempt to recognize the power differentials present and to understand how
they impinge upon what is sayable and doable in that specific
context' (1992:81). The desire of the liberatory teacher to
empower students to voice their silenced or delegitimated
experiences—in order to see how they have been dominated
by those with power—fails to see power itself as 'productive
and present in all contexts, regulating all discourses and social
interactions' (1992:83) even those that are liberatory.

Calls for students to publicly reveal or even confess information about their lives and cultures in the presence of oth-

ers—including teachers—can be not only voyeuristic but dangerous, a form of surveillance to see if students produce the right voice. When students speak or write, Orner asks, whose interests are served? Anneliese Kramer-Dahl (1996) raises similar questions in the context of her university composition and basic writing class:

> How can we assume that a pedagogical practice which asks students to make public information about their experiences and cultures in the presence of others, could ever grant them a safe, egalitarian place in which to speak? . . . Arguing for such a practice skirts the issue of who, in the classroom, has the authority to judge what kind of experience counts as relevant and what kind of reading of it is 'correct.' (1996:251)

In her examination of the politics of feminist identity in the university, Carmen Luke (1992) argues that the move to legitimate personal voice and critical classroom dialogue—encouraging women students, for example, to reveal their cultural histories to a male academic—'grossly underestimates the sexual politics that structure classroom encounters' (1992:37). Luke locates such unexamined issues of language and power in the very notions of authenticity and realism that continue to characterise student voice:

> Confessions of the self, particularly when naturalized as unmediated expressions of real experience, can be valorized as 'authentic' (and beyond critique) regardless of the cultural meanings (e.g., racism, sexism, or classism in minority subcultures) that structure those expressions and experiences. . . . Privileging experience as foundational to knowledge, or as a transparent window to the 'real,' denies its situatedness in discourses that constitute subjectivities in the first place, and that enable articulation of experience from discursively constructed subject positions (cf. Fuss 1989; Henriques *et al.* 1984;

> Walkerdine 1990). Both teacher and student subject
> are equally implicated in discursive networks. Stu-
> dents' articulation of 'real' experience and teachers'
> interpretive, emancipatory task *within* the institu-
> tional discourse of schooling do not reside outside
> of interlocking discourses and networks of institu-
> tionalized gender and power relations. (1992:37)

I have focused primarily on the central place of voice in
writing workshop and critical pedagogies rather than in
women's studies, cultural studies or feminist pedagogies of
difference which attempt to re-envision Freirian goals of liberation and social progress (Weiler 1994). Voice, however, has
also been employed and critiqued in a wider range of research contexts, including curriculum theory and teacher
education, where there is an impetus 'to understand curriculum as political, racial, gender, phenomenological, and autobiographical text' (Pinar 1997:82).

Andy Hargreaves (1996), for example, critiques the tendency to essentialise and eradicate difference in the literature on teacher's voice. 'This discourse works by selectively
appropriating particular empirical voices of predominantly
humanistic, child-centred teachers, then condensing them
into a singular voice, *the* teacher's voice, which becomes
representative of all teachers' (1996:13). Hargreaves is critical of the tendency to selectively appropriate and decon-
textualize 'only those voices that broadly echo our own'
(1996:13), rather than listen to voices that differ or even
offend, and situate those voices across a range of teaching
contexts. 'It is perhaps time to contextualize the study of
teachers' voices, knowledge, and experience more, and to
romanticize and moralize about teachers' voices in general
rather less' (1996:16).

While Hargreaves remains committed to representing
teachers' voices in educational research and practice, he argues against an apolitical presentation that simply celebrates
voice (much as I would for student writing). He emphasises
instead the need to re-present teacher voices critically and
contextually and ensure that many voices are selected, even

those that have discrepant things to say about teaching and learning.

While the multiple disciplinary locations in which voice has been critiqued are far too numerous to recount here, a proliferation of titles employing the prefix *re*, for example *Revisiting Voice* (Hargreaves 1996), *Rewriting Student Voice* (Lensmire 1998), *Reclaiming Voice* (USC 1997) indicates a widely recognised need to work with alternative methodological, pedagogical and theoretical frameworks. The critiques examined in this chapter make it clear that any re-conception of voice must, at the very least, attend more carefully to the social and historical contexts in which classrooms are located—not as abstract sets of relations—but as complex intersections of cultural histories, multiple identities, institutional constraints and shifting power relations between students and teachers and between students.

Ultimately, however, such critiques also raise serious questions about the adequacy of the metaphor of voice itself for the socially critical practices of writing I wish to develop in this book. If voice is an 'oppressive' and problematic construct, why use it? While multiple voices is 'a corrective move through pluralisation' (Kramer-Dahl 1996:256), full expression of multiple voices may not solve the problem of 'authenticity' and 'real' because voice itself is a metaphor of the body—located in the throat and vocal chords—and therefore difficult to disconnect from the body of the person writing.

Even when I rewrite voice as a socially constructed position in discourse and argue for a reconceived notion of *situated voice*, it is still difficult to disconnect the voice metaphor from discourses which locate it inside the person as authentic. While Orner is right that '[w]e must refuse the tendency to attribute 'authenticity' to people's voices when they speak from their own experience of difference, as if their speech were transparent and their understanding of their experience unchanging' (1992:86), I am not clear that even revised metaphors of voice can achieve this.

Lensmire's metaphoric reconception of *voice as project*, for example, is a case in point. If we take up his focus on *project*, we gain a 'sense of student voice as dynamic or in-process' (1998:278), as requiring development and crafting rather than being 'already-finished' or 'frozen at the beginning of the educational process' (1998:279). If we take up his focus on struggle, conflict and appropriation, we can more adequately represent the interactional and ideological complexities of writing classrooms. In the end, however, Lensmire's revision equivocates on the relationship between voice and self. While his concern is not to reduce self to voice, his reconception assumes that 'voice is an aspect of the self but not the whole self' (1998:287). This leaves me asking, which part, and with what consequences?—particularly when he remains committed in his conclusion to (a somewhat romantic) 'flourishing of student voices in school' (1998:261).

As a feminist linguist and critical discourse analyst who takes seriously the power of metaphors to shape what it is possible to think, it seems to me more prudent at this point in time to *not* use the metaphor of voice. For despite a million useful critiques and revisions, the metaphor itself stays intact when we continue to use and reuse it—even qualify it as *situated voice*. This is not to dismiss its significance, history or even some of the goals associated with its use in a number of critical, democratic and emancipatory projects. It is to argue that we need other discursive means to disrupt the link between person and voice—and voice and authentic experience.

FROM VOICE TO STORY

Madeleine Grumet (1990), dissatisfied with the use of voice as a metaphor for feminist theory and pedagogy, offers a more complex construction, consisting of three elements: situation, narrative and interpretation.

> The first, situation, acknowledges that we tell our story as a speech event that involves the social, cultural and political relations in and to which we speak. Narrative, or narratives as I prefer, invites all the specificity, presence and power that the sym-

bolic and semiotic registers of our speaking can
provide. And interpretation provides another voice,
a reflexive and more distant one. (1990:281–2)

In Grumet's conception no element of this trio is privileged;
all are required for a 'dynamic, reflective, and finally collaborative version of voice' that might 'generate new ways of
teaching and schooling' (1990:282). In the context of a pedagogy of writing, I would argue this movement from voice to
story is significant—both in terms of metaphor and practice.

Metaphorically, story allows a more textual orientation
than voice, a closer attention to what is written (rather than
she who has written)—to the actual text—and the contexts
in which it is produced. Where voice relies on metaphors of
sound and speech, without necessarily invoking either context or meaning, story invokes a text, a syntax and a structure of telling. Metaphors of speech, because they imply
delivery by a human voice, act discursively to naturalise
personal writing as more authentic 'personal, individual, spon-
taneous, natural, truthful, involved, emotional, real' (Gilbert
1990:60–1). Metaphors of story, by contrast, can be used to
disrupt the links between the personal and the authentic.

The last ten years have seen a burgeoning interest in
story and narrative across a wide range of disciplinary contexts (education, composition, sociology, literacy) as a framework for understanding the construction of knowledge in
relation to lived experience (Tierney and Lincoln 1997). While
the range of theorising on narrative as a research methodology, as a pedagogy, and as a mode of curriculum inquiry is far
too extensive to explore here (see, for example, Thomson 1997–
98a), we can identify some features that are useful to the
relocated notion of the personal I wish to work with in this
book.

Stories are specific rather than abstract, they 'arise out of
specific rhetorical situations, cultural contexts and historical
moments: they are relative to time, place, gender, race and
ideology (Summerfield 1994:180). Stories do not tell single
truths, but rather represent a truth, a perspective, a particular
way of seeing experience and naming it. Stories are partial,

they are located rather than universal, they are a representation of experience rather than the same thing as experience itself ('not authentic').

Such perspectives bring a critical lens to the production and enactment of texts and suggest a whole new set of educational practices. These include a greater self-consciousness about how narratives are told, how they are made, how they might be written differently, how they support, undermine and struggle with other stories, how their writing affects both the teller and the told.

My preference for story over voice then, is linguistic, political and educational. The construct of narrative allows for a kind of specificity, agency and analysis that constructs of voice do not. The implications for a critical writing pedagogy are explored in the next four chapters where I demonstrate in particular how metaphors of textuality

- allow a clearer separation between the writer's life and the experience she is writing about;
- make the labour of the writer more visible, less naturalised and therefore more accessible to the learner;
- treat stories as a learned cultural practice, so that the process of production and the stories produced can be unpicked, examined and analysed rather than just celebrated or surveilled for the right/wrong voice.

RELOCATING TRANSFORMATION

At the centre of many critical and liberatory pedagogies of voice is a dissatisfaction with the status quo—with educational practices which silence the experiences of large numbers of students and reproduce social relations of inequity. The imperative to give space to student voice has been founded on the assumption that to do so will improve things and contribute to universal goals of liberation and social transformation.

The difficulties of putting into practice such universal goals is highlighted by Kathleen Weiler (1994) in her critique of Freire's classic liberatory pedagogy. Her feminist rewriting does 'not reject the goals of justice, the end of oppression, and liberation, but frames them more specifically' (1994:14), addressing 'the contradictions and tensions within social settings in which overlapping forms of oppression exist' (1994:16).

In a similar move, I would argue here for a more situated, localised understanding of the transformative power of writing, still grounded in a vision of social change but relocated outside metaphors of voice and universal calls for social transformation. I would disconnect the personal from notions of transformation that are too large, too self-congratulatory and have too much of the conversion narrative about them. Instead I am interested in the ways a writer's personal experience can be represented in text, in the shifts in subjectivity that are made possible through rewriting and re-imagining the text. Within such a pedagogy the 'personal' is based on a poststructuralist notion of subjectivity rather than an essential, singular self. Following Weedon (1987), I understand that subjectivity

> to refer to the conscious and unconscious thoughts and emotions of the individual, her sense of herself and her ways of understanding her relation to the world. Humanist discourses presuppose an essence at the heart of the individual which is unique, fixed and coherent and which makes her what she is. . . . [P]oststructuralism proposes a subjectivity which is precarious, contradictory and in process, constantly being reconstituted in discourse each time we think or speak. (1987:32–3)

The significance of this conception for writing is that it opens up 'the personal' to change (a less grand, more provisional term than transformation). It allows us to imagine the possibility of rewriting the multiple and contradictory subject positions we occupy and/or bringing into being new positions to sit alongside the old. It allows 'the possibilities of stories of resistance, not determinism, and of new, transformed selves' (Threadgold 1996:291).

> Although the subject in poststructuralism is socially constructed in discursive practices, she none the less exists as a thinking, feeling subject and social agent, capable of resistance and innovations produced out of the clash between contradictory subject positions and practices. She is also a subject able to reflect upon the discursive relations which constitute her and the society in which she lives, and able to choose from the options available. (Weedon 1987:125)

This notion that subjectivities are discursively constructed and can therefore be reconstructed seems to me a productive ground for rethinking a pedagogy of the personal that promotes agency. Pinar (1997) argues, in a similar vein, that because we live in a discursive world, 'the process of education requires narrative voices which disclose the political character of language and the rhetorical features of social change. "There must be some way outta here" and the passage is discursive' (1997:94).

In the remainder of this chapter I explore the transformative possibilities of writing the personal, by turning to Foucault's notion of self-writing, not as confession but as intertextual borrowing and care of self, and to Kress' social semiotic theory of representation, where writing is seen as a design for both subjectivity and text.

WRITING THE SELF: FOUCAULT

Foucault's reflections on self-writing are part of a series of studies on the 'practices of the self' in Greco–Roman culture during the first two centuries of the empire. Such practices can be understood more broadly to be concerned with the government of self, 'an exercise of self upon self by which one tries to work out, to transform one's self and to attain a certain mode of being' (Foucault 1988:2).

Such work upon the self is not simply to be understood as a kind of liberation. Distrustful of the general theme of liberation, Foucault takes a more cautious position, less reliant on metaphors of liberation from repressive mechanisms and more focused on Greco–Roman practices of freedom—ways of acting and behaving ethically through a caring for the self.

Although the idea of care for self will later become suspect when read through discourses of Christianity, the Greeks and Romans understood a care for one's self to be social (not simply selfish) and beneficial to others.

> For the Greeks it is not because it is care for others that it is ethical. Care for self is ethical in itself, but it implies complex relations with others, in the measure where this ethos of freedom is always a way of caring for others. (Foucault 1988:7)

The act of self-writing, within this conception, is seen as an essential practice in the care and training of the self, whereby 'the writer constitutes his own identity through this recollection of things said' (Foucault 1997:240). '[T]hese practices are nevertheless not something that the individual invents by himself. They are patterns that he finds in his culture and which are proposed, suggested and imposed on him by his culture, his society and his social group' (Foucault 1988:11).

This interface between the personal and the social—between the historical, social, cultural uses of language and the ways these shape and are shaped by the writer—are most evident in the practice described by Foucault as *hupomnemata*, personal notebooks used in the first and second centuries to care for and develop the self. These notebooks contained quotations, fragments of works read, actions witnessed, arguments, reflections, 'a material memory of things read, heard, thought' (1997:236) which one might 'read, reread, meditate, converse with oneself and others' (1997:237). Although they were personal notebooks, they were not intimate journals or narratives of spiritual experience found in later Christian literature:

> their objective is not to bring into the light the *arcana consientiae* for which confession—oral or written—has a purifying value. The movement that they seek to effect is the inverse of that; it is not a matter of pursuing the unsayable, nor of revealing the hidden, nor of saying the unsaid, but on the contrary of capturing the already-said, of reassembling what one could hear or read, and this for an end that is nothing less than the constitution of the self. (1997:237)

This understanding of self-writing—its role in constituting the self—avoids the slippage between personal experience and authentic truth critiqued above in my discussion of voice. The act of writing for oneself or about oneself is not simply seen as a focus on the private, as a site of confession and intimate knowledge. The personal, as Patricia Williams (1991: 93) writes, 'is not the same as 'private': the personal is often merely the highly particular'.

Using this same example of the *hupomnemata*, Lensmire (1998) argues that Foucault's distinction between these earlier (Greek) and later (Christian) uses of notebooks is analogous to the contrast he draws between a workshop conception of voice and his alternative—in particular the use of appropriation.

Lensmire's notion of appropriation emphasises the activity of the self in relation to the cultural resources available. Appropriation involves a taking over of those resources—experiences, language, histories, stories—and reworking them. This labour, according to Lensmire, crafts a self and a voice, a voice which is dependent on the voices of others who precede the writer but which is also remade by the writer as she takes over the language of others. 'In crafting her voice, the individual responds to and transforms the utterances of others in the production of her own speaking and writing' (Lensmire 1998:280).

While I prefer Foucault's use of self-writing and its more textual orientation (ie, writing a self) to Lensmire's use of voice, the question of how the writing operates to remake and relocate a writer's subjectivity still needs to be addressed more fully. To do so, I turn to Kress' social semiotic theory of representation. This is a theory where the writer's 'subjectivity [is placed] in the center, between social and cultural possibilities, and it forces, on the one hand, available resources and structures of power and, on the other, the individual's action in the making of signs' (Kress 1996:238).

REWRITING THE SELF: KRESS

In Kress' social semiotic theory of representation, the making of signs—the making of writing—is seen as an action that can be explained in terms of social structures and cultural systems. Within this conception the writer is seen as an experienced maker of signs who produces and transforms signs. An intimate and reciprocal relationship is posited between the forms of representation—the signs the writer uses—and the forms of subjectivity produced.

With regard to the sign itself, Kress argues there is a motivated conjunction of form (signifier) and meaning (signified). Makers of signs use the most apt forms of expression for their meaning, rather than simply arbitrary ones. To illustrate the way signs are motivated conjunctions of meaning and form, Kress uses the example of the three-year-old child who uses two circles to represent a car. For this child, the car is primarily defined by the criterial aspect of having wheels and wheels are plausibly represented by circles—both in terms of their visual appearance and the circular motion of drawing the wheels and repeating the action of the wheels going around. The 'whole object' or experience, the car in this instance, can never be fully represented. Only certain criterial aspects can be represented in the most apt, plausible fashion using the resources that are available.

While adults have a rich set of cultural resources with which to make signs, they are also constrained in making signs because they are aware (consciously or unconsciously) of the conventionally established modes of making meaning which the culture values. Young children, by contrast, have both more and less freedom of expression—more because they have not yet learned to confine the making of signs to conventionally established modes of sign making—less because the resources available to them are less developed. Although children initially do not make the same distinctions in sign making as the adult culture around them, as they are drawn into culture, the resources available to them in social conventionalised forms become more what the culture values.

Crucially, for both adults and children, selecting signs from the available resources involves a remaking, however slight that may be. That is, the activity of using the resources can be viewed as transformative activity, not simply as imitation or repetition but as remaking. In this conception, Kress differs from linguists who treat the language system as independent of the writer and the role of the writer as a fairly mechanical, inert one. His view, based on a critique of the dominant hegemonic reading of Saussure—in particular the ahistorical, synchronic aspects of Saussure's theory—'sees language as predominantly a socially, culturally, and historically produced system' (Kress 1996:236). In using that system (and its meanings which are never value-free) the writer is affected.

The writer, then, is at the same time a user of language and also a (re)maker 'of that system of representation, out of their social and cultural histories and . . . their affective dispositions' (1996:236):

> the systems of representation are both the product of individual actions and the effect of the socially and culturally available resources. The systems of representation of any social and cultural group are the effects of the collective actions of individual makers of signs. Social and individual semiotic,

communicative, and representational activities are
thus linked in a complex but tightly integrated mesh.
(1996:237)

For Kress, however, the act of writing is not only a transformative practice through which we constantly refashion our
representations; it also involves a transformation of the writer/
sign maker's subjectivity. The writer's action in making new
signs out of existing representational resources continually
alters the conceptual repertoire of the individual and, in doing
so, alters the individual's subjectivity. The student who uses
representational resources to produce a poem and the child
who uses circles to represent a car are, in a sense, not the
same individuals as they were before. Their potential for
producing meaning has both increased and altered. A change
has occurred in who they are and who they can be.

> Changed subjectivities entail changed potentials for
> identity—where 'identity' indicates the production
> of a relatively stable external display, a 'persona,' from
> a particular configuration of internal resources or
> states, out of a given subjectivity. (Kress 1996: 237)

There is the added dimension of response. If the child's circles
or the student's poem gets a response, it is praised for certain
things and ignored for others; this further shapes the set of
resources available—both what counts as a car or poem and
how the writer sees her capacity to produce those resources.
Forms of communication which are not publicly acknowledged or valued tend to be less developed and less articulated
than those which are. Existing relationships of power also
govern which meanings and metaphors dominate and pass
into semiotic systems as natural.

Given this 'mutually interacting and interdependent' relationship between 'modes of representation' and 'subjectivity'
(Kress 1996:237), there are crucial implications for the development of writing pedagogies. That is, forms of pedagogies

can also be seen as *designs* for subjectivities, where different modes and potentials of meaning making imply different potentials for the formation of subjectivities.

The concept of design has been further developed by Kress in dialogue with Australian, American and British colleagues as the basis on which to develop a pedagogy of multiliteracies (New London Group 1996). The New London pedagogical framework consists of three interactive components: available designs (historically and culturally received patterns of meaning), designing (the process of making and remaking) and the redesigned (a transformed meaning).

Within this framework, meaning makers (writers, in this instance) use available designs to make meaning. The outcome of their designing is seen to be a new meaning (the redesigned), through which they remake themselves. The redesigned, in turn, (which we can think of as a text) becomes a new available design, a new meaning making resource. It is through the processes of designing that writers produce new representations of reality and at the same time remake themselves—that is, reconstruct and renegotiate their identities. Not only is the redesigned (the text) a product of human agency, in such a paradigm, it is also 'evidence of the ways in which the active intervention in the world that is Designing has transformed the designer' (New London Group 1996:76).

Such notions of design and transformation are productive for a critical writing pedagogy committed to relocating the personal—to asserting the power of writing to transform the text and the way experience is viewed. Such notions avoid universal claims, allow agency and keep the personal highly specific (rather than private). Writing, in short, is never simply a skill but deeply constitutive of subjectivity. Writing a self, turning it into a textual artefact, makes it productively useable in ways in which it was not prior to it being written down. In chapter 3, I exemplify this notion of writing as a site of both subjectivity and text formation in my work with older women. I examine, in particular, how the personal is fashioned out of a complex set of cultural resources that both shape the writer and are shaped by her.

CHAPTER THREE

Stories of Ageing

❖

Bella entered the writing workshop a woman in grief. Her husband had died thirteen months earlier, and she continued to mourn his absence as she marked the one-year anniversary of his death, a ritualised milestone in her Jewish culture. Each week in the workshop Bella cried easily, as if the slightest touch of her skin could make her tears overflow. I suggested she consider writing about her husband's death, as the act of writing might help, and certainly would not be more difficult than her present pain. To confront death by constructing a narrative of dying, however, is to break a cultural silence that refuses death as part of life.

In this chapter I explore writing strategies developed in five 'stories of ageing' writing workshops conducted between 1993 and 1999. Initially, 'stories of ageing' projects were conducted by myself and Susan Feldman, director of the Alma Unit on Women and Ageing at the University of Melbourne. From 1997 to 1999 our work was extended and redeveloped as an Australian Council Research Grant with Terry Threadgold of Monash University, Melbourne. This was a three-year longitudinal study which examined change in the lives and the concerns of women aged 70–85 living outside institutional care. Working as a team with approximately forty women in workshop settings, we extended our ways of working with autobiographical stories to include video diary workshop as well as writing workshop methodologies, where women both filmed and wrote their stories of ageing. The purpose of the project was to confront the narrow range of negative images of ageing pervasive in our culture and to produce new stories written from the perspective of the older woman.

Bella not only agreed but seemed physically transformed when she returned with her story the following week. The black circles under her eyes had lightened and her white streaked hair was pushed back with a dramatic flair as she read her text aloud to the group.

It was late Friday afternoon and the sun was going down. I set the table for Shabbat. The white table-cloth, the candles, the Israeli Shabbat plate Irene gave us, the velvet cover for the challot. Sam watched as I went through the ritual of lighting the candles and we wished each other Shabbat Shalom. I knew he was pleased.

We started our last meal. He ate the fish our friend Sula had cooked his favourite way. He en-joyed eating it and had to ring to thank her. For the rest of his last conscious evening he was his usual sweet self. We sat at the table and talked. He was sorry for losing his patience earlier and apologised. He was frightened of losing his mind and please would I forgive him. I hugged him and reassured him I was with him in whatever he did.

He went to bed. I gave him his sleeping pill and as every night before falling asleep he said, 'Darling another day together—thank you.' We kissed and soon he was asleep. I read for a while and went to sleep next to Sam.

When I woke up some time later, Sam was lay-ing across my bed—he could not move or talk, he just looked at me with wide opened eyes. I tried to shift him but could not do it. A nurse arrived and we put him back in his bed. He was conscious and restless. The doctor ordered a Valium injection which calmed him down and he fell asleep.

When he awoke on Saturday morning, he was conscious and responded to requests, but did not speak any more. . . . I knew that he was dying and that I could not do more than stay with him. I was calm. I knew that this was the end and that these moments would stay with me as long as I lived. I needed to remember every one of them, every breath, every change. I lay next to him fully dressed and watched him. I called his name. He opened his eyes—he could hear me. His mouth was dry and I put some soothing lotion on it. I listened to his breath, felt his pulse, touched his body. I lost sense of time and space. I felt removed from everything and everybody. There was only Sam and I. I remember his breath becoming slower, the silences becoming longer and then it stopped. Sam was dead.

I touched his face and kissed him. He was warm and soft. I do not remember crying. I stayed alone in the room until he was taken away. The last I saw of Sam was the long plastic black bag in which he was carried out. Somebody tore the blouse I was wearing. I was left alone. There was nothing for me to do, Sam had arranged all the formalities ahead of time. I vaguely remember the funeral. I felt and still feel that part of me died with Sam.

As researchers, we were particularly interested in the way dominant narratives prevent stories such as Bella's from being told and how, by interrupting these, it is possible for older women to tell other stories (Farrell *et al.* 2000). In poststructuralist terms, the relation between lived and imagined stories is significant. The stories we tell provide the frameworks through which we act (Lyotard 1984). Stories are interpretive resources for dealing with the everyday world and for taking ourselves up within the cultural storylines available to us (Davies 1994; Gilbert 1993a). Such notions provide a way to theorise ageing as a changing, contradictory and gendered process and the ageing woman as positioned within the categories our dominant narratives have provided (Kamler and Feldman 1995). Ageing women are not seen as passively shaped by others but as capable of taking up discourses through which they are shaped and through which they may reshape themselves.

Of course, it is not easy to tell stories of ageing outside dominant discourses of loss and pain (Kamler 1996). As ageing inevitably involves loss: of loved ones, partners, friends; of beauty and youthful appearance; of position in the workforce and attendant power and influence, it is easier to think of ageing as a time of disintegration and uselessness. It is also easy to stereotype older women as a singular group, to expect that they all experience the ageing process in the same way. The stories of ageing project challenged these positions by theorising ageing as an embodied process of change and by positioning ageing women as agents and collaborators in intellectual work (Feldman *et al.* 1998). In this, it moves in the same direction as other feminist poststructuralist work on ageism and ageing (Laws 1995; Ray 1996).

Pedagogically, the project was structured to create a writing workshop space that allowed women to identify a range of concerns from their own local and specific perspectives as ageing women, much as Bella did. Her story constructs the passing of life as an intimacy within a loving marriage. It is a highly crafted text—rather than an anguished outpouring of self—which disrupts dominant narratives of death as frightening. The images are soft and romantic, there is a tenderness in lying beside Sam, a sensuousness in applying the soothing lotion to his lips, in touching his soft skin and in the final kisses. This is a moment within the pain of loss that is almost safe—a stark contrast to the cold plastic bag in which Sam is taken away or the more violent rending of Bella's garment—a tradition within Judaism to embody the beginning of the mourning period.

The stories of ageing workshops were designed using principles from Frigga Haug's (1987) memory work, a method of inquiry which is collective and deconstructive. Through group processes of drafting, revising and theorising, women such as Bella developed not only new writing skills, but a critical understanding of the discursive processes that shape older women's lives and other people's perceptions of them. The workshops differed from Haug's in that we worked for a much shorter period of time with women who did not identify as academic or feminist and did not engage in poststructuralist reading on discourse, language and subjectivity, as is often the case in studies which utilise variations of memory work (eg, Davies 1994; Kippax *et al.* 1988).

Typically, we met with groups of ten to twelve women weekly in two–hour workshops over a six- to eight-week period. The women brought to the project a mix of histories, both personal and professional, and represented a predominantly white, middle to lower middle-class population from a range of Eastern European to Anglo-Celtic origins, with one Filipina participant. Their participation in the project was understood by the women as part of a collaborative exchange: they would learn new strategics for crafting and developing writing, and we, the researchers, would gain new understandings of ageing from their writing. What we understood less well, initially, was that the women's writing would also become a site for producing new signs—new metaphors, new ways of speaking about ageing—*and* new forms of subjectivity. The transformative nature of this process can best be exemplified by looking more closely at the production of Bella's text.

Bella's story presented an enormous challenge to our goal of separating the personal from its textual representation because Bella was, so to speak, enmeshed in her text and indistinguishable from it. Before reading aloud to the group Bella announced 'I know this writing is not supposed to be therapy, but for me it was therapeutic'. Then as she read she fought tears. She had practised reading the story in front of the mirror so she wouldn't cry and was angry with herself when the tears came. The other women reached out in support, touching her shoulder, making words of comfort and appreciation for her courage to write about this time of grief.

Without being insensitive to Bella's pain or to the memories of loss engendered in the group, I struggled with the fine line between personal writing and therapy. I wanted to allow the sympathy and full engagement with Bella's positioning as grieving widow, but I was also looking for a discursive space to move forward, a space where I would *not* be positioned as therapist and could treat the experience written on the page as a representation (and a crafted one at that) of Bella's loss, not the same as the loss itself. That is, it was a particular way of representing her experience of Sam's death, one which could be examined and rewritten differently.

I asked Bella if she also wanted to treat this writing as text, as an object which we could ask questions of and interact with critically. In retrospect, this was a significant move, as it allowed Bella the choice and also the possibility of separating out from the narrative she had constructed. I was struck by a number of absences in her text that we might address, in particular, the primary focus on the husband's goodness and the lack of naming of the wife's love and generosity in providing him with a 'good death'. I was surprised when Bella said yes. The writing was therapeutic, as she had said, but she wanted to do more work. In subsequent weeks Bella made a few changes, but the most interesting was the addition of a line to the very end of her text:

> If there is anything that lessens my pain, it is the feeling that my being with him until the end gave him the strength he needed and that he died surrounded by love and care.

This revision is significant in accomplishing a slightly different understanding of Bella's agency in accomplishing a peaceful death for her husband. That revision, as I argued in chapter 2, can be seen not only as a change to text, but as achieving a shift in the writer's subjectivity. Writing the story literally stimulated a change of bodily tissue, a lifting of darkness from Bella's shoulders and eyes, an easing of her pain. It created a discursive space for her to explore her loss textually and extended the semiotic resources available for speaking about taboo topics such as death. The workshop space allowed a different kind of cultural regulation and making of signs—and in that making, a remaking of self. Importantly, the text also accomplished a repositioning of Bella within the group, so that she was freed in subsequent weeks to construct a variety of textual positionings other than 'grieving widow' and participate as a more engaged reader of others' texts, less consumed with her own pain and more attuned to others.

In the remainder of this chapter I make visible some of the workshop practices that shaped texts such as Bella's. I focus on how these practices, while initially located within process writing pedagogies, have been relocated within a more critical framework that foregrounds issues of representation, power and positioning. Within such a framework, the aim is *not* to reveal the truth of the writer's personal experiences or express who they *really* are, their authentic voice. It is to understand that in writing subjectivity may be defined, contested and remade (Kamler 1995b).

Given my history as a writing teacher, the process of relocating these practices has involved a rewriting of what I have known. Sometimes the shifts have been subtle, sometimes not, but the most dramatic change has been to reconceptualise writing pedagogy as a design for effective text production *and* the production of subjectivity (Kress 1996; New London Group 1996). Such a frame requires a greater self-consciousness about the material effects of writing on bodies and minds. It also requires a different understanding of the individual writer, the questions we might ask of her text and the kinds of purposes writing might serve.

WRITING AS CRITIQUE: THE WRITING CONFERENCE RELOCATED

The stories of ageing workshops were structured so that each week the women brought a piece of writing which they read aloud for response and critique. Reading aloud gives the writer distance from the experience being written about. Asking critical questions helps the writer see that her text is a representation of experience—*not* the same as experience itself.

To foster this distancing, we developed a group conference strategy using a critical set of questions to relocate the personal. We did not ask writers which part they liked best or what person they identified with or how they felt about the writing, as often occurs in process workshops. Instead, we tried *not* to highlight how the reader responded to the writer's life. We placed the focus on the textual practice not the person, on the writing as a representation. Some of our questions included the following:

- What is powerful in the writing? Identify an image, line, metaphor, or representation of person that is powerful.
- What is omitted? Who/what is absent and/or hinted at or overgeneralised?
- What clichés are used to gloss over experience, facts, feelings?
- What doesn't fit? What contradictions, if any, emerge?
- What aspects/issues of ageing are constructed/concealed?
- What common issues, experiences, storylines do the texts have in common?

These are not necessarily *the* best questions and we never asked a group to attend to all of these at any one time. The questions are suggestive, however, of a different frame for reading text than that constructed by Murray's process paradigm. Our approach, in fact, can be understood as a relocating of Murray's notion of conferencing using poststructuralist feminist theorising (Haug 1987).

> It's not a question of throwing out the innovations of teachers like Elbow and Murray or of shutting down the voices and personal experiences of students; rather, it's a question of relocating those practices and interests in a different theoretical context—getting a larger sense of what produces them and of what the writing based in them should do. (Jarratt 1991:113)

Murray (1982) conceives the writing conference as a conversation between teacher and student, where the purpose is not to correct or surveil the text—not to fix it up to the teachers' satisfaction—but to see how it works and consider how it might work differently. Murray's metaphor for the site of this interaction is the workbench, where craftspersons meet to shape the text.

I think I've begun to learn the right questions to ask at the beginning of a writing conference.

'What did you learn from this piece of writing?'
'What do you intend to do in the next draft?'
'What surprised you in the draft?'
'Where is the piece of writing taking you?'
'What do you like best in the piece of writing?'
'What questions do you have of me?'

I feel as if I have been searching for the right questions, questions which would establish a tone of master and apprentice, no, the voice of a fellow craftsman having a conversation about a piece of work, writer to writer, neither praise nor criticism but questions which imply further drafts, questions which draw helpful comments out of the student writer. (Murray 1982:159)

Such conversations with students about their texts have been characterised by Lensmire (1994:38) as interviews, where the teacher asks questions about the writing to understand how students are attempting to solve writing problems and to support them in their efforts. A major value of such conversations is that they create a different type of agency than that normally attributed to student writers. A major weakness is that they may also create a reluctance by teachers to interfere with the writer's personal voice.

A great deal of controversy has centred on the role of the teacher and the kinds of questions she asks in conference. In Australia, a particularly harsh critique was developed by advocates of genre approaches to writing (eg, Painter and Martin 1986), attacking in particular, the nondirective role of the progressive writing teacher in the writing conference. While I agree that questions advocated by writing workshop approaches are often too nondirective—too uncritical—too nonspecific with regard to the genre being constructed, this is no reason to throw out the conference structure itself. Theoretically, the conference is a powerful interactive structure for language learning, consistent with Vygostsky's (1978) notion of learning in the zone of proximal development and Bruner's notion of scaffolding the learner's understanding (Ninio and Bruner 1978).

The understandings that are scaffolded, however, depend on the teacher's notion of text and the relationship between text and experience, something Murray never theorised from the humanist paradigm in which he operated. If the teacher treats the text as truth, as the *real* expression of the individual writer (whose identity is received, unitary and stable), then she is loathe to touch it. She can create no space to intervene and no rationale for why she should meddle with 'you'. After all, she is not your therapist, nor is she qualified to be so.

But if she understands that the text is not 'you'—that it is from you but is not the same as 'you'—that it represents a particular way of telling your experience—a representation— a construct—then a different curiosity can be aroused in the conference. What aspects of experience have you selected? Why have you selected these? And what have you left out? Not why in the sense of your psyche but in terms of your multiple locations in a number of discursive practices. The teacher can become interested in the text you have created and can begin to work with you to ask questions of it. She may even use the space to produce a number of different readings and demonstrate the multiple and contradictory effects one text can have.

In the years following the 'Till Death Do Us Part' episode (see chapter 1) when I was looking for alternate ways to theorise the writing conference, I was strongly influenced by Haug's (1987) poststructuralist methodology, in particular, her view of analysing stories as a practice of active change. Haug pays close attention to detail in writing, to focusing on a particular situation, rather than life in its entirety. She sees 'what is "not" said as interesting, and the fact that it is not said as important (Haug 1987:65); she attempts to interrogate contradictions in language as traces of the contradictions in our lives and as a means of questioning the taken for granted.

Her influence is seen in the questions we developed in the stories of ageing workshops. Our focus on image or metaphor keeps the focus on language, on the choices made and the fact that these are selections. It makes the first reading self-conscious with regard to structure, but it also creates a space to affirm what writers have achieved. Once the women in the workshops began to look for images, these became productive points for discussing new metaphors—grey hair as a symbol of no intellect, tightrope walking at the end of one's career, a compass for finding one's way at the end of her life.

The questions on absence were particularly powerful in helping the women understand that what is omitted may be as important as what is included. If writing involves selection, we can ask what is *not* represented and thereby investigate how writing silences some aspects of experience (consciously or unconsciously) and privileges others. Absences are about what cannot be said or what it is difficult to say, not because of a reluctance to reveal personal secrets, but because dominant narratives and/or one's discursive positioning make it difficult to imagine other positions from which to speak or write.

Bella's story, at the beginning of the chapter, demonstrates the effects of working explicitly with absences around the experience of death. Ruth's story confronts the cultural silence that often surrounds the ageing woman's body. As an ageing woman, Ruth lives in a culture that reveres the youthful body and fears anything to do with wrinkles and gravity. Her text, however, positions the reader to look in the mirror with her and examine the changes to her body.

> Basically I'm a slob. I'm happiest wearing clothes that are two sizes too big for me thus eradicating the constant preoccupation with losing weight. Add to this the fact that I take longer to reach decisions and my movements are slower and you can begin to realise that getting ready to go out has become a major operation. Years ago, the phone would ring and ten minutes later I would be out the door showered and dressed. Nowadays, I need plenty of notice and at least an hour's preparation time before I can face the world.

First there is the hair. My hair is white-grey and short and therefore the timing of the haircut becomes crucial. A day too late, it looks straggly and a day too early, it's tough looking. The hair cut needs precision timing, making appointments and then meeting that time whether you feel like it or not. One does not annoy one's hairdresser. Too much hangs on his good humour. He has such easy methods of punishing those who cross him; he holds the scissors after all.

Then there is the waxing. That's a weekly affair. Nature is perverse; while other parts of the body are shedding hair at an alarming rate, the chin blooms with increasing rapidity. Where facial hair is concerned, minutes count. What in the morning appears to be virgin chin, suddenly sprouts fine little ringlets by the afternoon. These little treasures require the assistance of my strongest glasses plus a proper magnifying mirror and just the right light. If the sun is not out, forget it, I can't find them. I console myself with the belief that my friends' eyesight is no longer what it was either . . .

Finally, I'm into the make up. It's really a put on and wipe off exercise. I need an even colour to hide the brown spots and at the same time I know that too much camouflage brings the 'older woman' perilously close to looking like a clown. The application of make up requires patient loving care, a good dose of vanity and most importantly the belief that it will help. More often than not, rather than deal with this trauma, I opt for the natural look and smear some moisturiser on my face. Who am I kidding? By this time I look like a grease pot, oil leaking from the too open pores. Much blotting with tissues ensues.

At last I'm answering the door. I can read the disapproval on my friend's face. She is desperately trying to find something nice to say about the way I look. It's not easy for her, I can sense that, and I feel sorry for her, for suddenly I don't really care that much anyway. It's a liberating feeling. I'm going out with a friend to see a good film and perhaps dinner afterwards. We will chat and argue over countless events, books and family. We will feel stimulated and alive. Perhaps the passion does not reach the dizzying heights of a time now past, but it will warm and sustain us nevertheless.

The discussion which scaffolded Ruth's story focused on the numerous cultural practices which construct ageing women as invisible. The women talked about *not* feeling old, *not* looking their age, and the startling disjunction between the way they looked and felt, described by Featherstone and Hepworth (1991) as a 'mask of ageing'. The face appears as a mask which cannot be removed, which is subject to the public gaze and cultural judgment; below the ageing surface, a sense of youthful identity is maintained, a continuous sense of the self that does not match the reflection in the mirror. To help women find language to talk about their ageing bodies, we set the writing exercise 'When I look in the mirror I see', and asked them to focus on what they did see, rather than on what they did not.

Ruth's response positions the older woman within discourses of femininity and youth, where beauty and physical appearance are foregrounded as a measure of woman's social worth. What her story disrupts is the defining power of those physical changes. We see her struggle with cutting, waxing and plucking her body to fit the ideal, but we know her commitment is only partial. What she constructs instead is a new discursive space, a way of detailing the changes while staying separate from them. In that space, she positions her reader to laugh both at the conventions and at her feeble attempt to conform to them.

She forces us to see the hair on her chin, rather than give us leave to notice those hairs and impose the usual negative cultural judgment. Although the bodily changes are ugly to her, she refuses camouflage. She will not pass for young, and in her refusal disrupts the cultural assumption that looking younger than one's years is to be admired. Through the details of her story, she exposes our complicity as women in trying to control our ageing body parts, but relocates this

desire within a number of marginalising cultural practices
(Kamler and Feldman 1995). The dialogue and conversation
in and around such texts thus lead older women to extend
their cultural resources, to ask questions about the common
storylines emerging across their texts and rewrite these as
discursive practices which effect the writer's body and mind.

WRITING AS REPRESENTATION: TELLING FACTS RELOCATED

An important component of the workshops was our focus on
selection and representation, on the fact that the details a
writer selects are a construct which give greater power (viv-
idness, engagement) to a narrative, but not necessarily greater
truth. One way we tried to interrupt the women's practiced
ways of telling about their experience as truth was to follow
Haug's (1987) procedure of writing in the third person, as if
the story were about someone else. We asked the women to
write with detail and kept the workshop focus on textuality
and crafting. It was then possible to ask questions about
what was represented and imagine other possibilities, rather
than be glued to the details.

In the early weeks of the workshops, however, women often resisted foregrounding their own experiences because, as
they later discussed with us, women of their generation had
been actively discouraged from talking about themselves. One
strategy we developed was to ask the women to write about
everyday practices. By encouraging them to attend to the detail
of what appeared to them at first to be 'uninteresting' and
'boring', we gave them tools with which to reimagine their
everyday lives and their own subject positions in ordinary spaces.

The importance of detail in writing about everyday lives
has been argued by a number of writing workshop advocates
(Murray 1982a, 1985; Graves 1983; Macrorie 1980). The 'Till
Death Do Us Part' story, however, demonstrates that detail
in itself, dislocated from a critical sense of how texts build
relations of power, can be dangerous. Simply writing more
and more detail can produce meanings that are problematic,

sometimes abhorrent (Gilbert 1993a). Our intervention was to relocate such strategies in poststructuralist understandings of text and language; where text is treated as a representation of experience and the details provide 'a stance, a perspective, an angle, in this version, this representation' (Summerfield 1994:187).

We developed a number of strategies to build such understandings. One was to work with visual images and ask questions about them. We showed, for example, a picture of four people in their seventies, two men and two women, one seated in a wheel chair, the others on a bench. In the background are windows with bars suggesting some institutional setting. We asked questions of the picture. Who are these people? How do you know? What is their relationship to one another? Are they two couples? If so, who goes with whom? Are there other possibilities, other combinations? And why is the woman in the wheelchair laughing? Such questions encouraged the production of narrative, close attention to visual detail and an articulation of which details produced particular readings of the picture.

Having established a number of possible storylines, we then played with reframing the picture. We covered the woman in the wheelchair so that the picture now showed a woman surrounded by two men. How did this change the possible set of relationships, we asked? What about when we covered the man at the end, leaving one man surrounded by two women? Or when we divided the foursome into two couples and looked at each separately. How did the story change with each reframing, each deliberate inclusion and exclusion? What new meanings were being created? This kind of visual work alerted the women to the narrative possibilities of experience and the power of detail in each narrative production they made.

A second strategy we called telling facts, after Ken Macrorie's (1980) exercise to help writers find the specific facts that lie behind a generalisation. With a stronger focus on facts as representation, not truth, we modelled a number of texts where writers included the details that 'tell'. One of these was written by a writer whose general statement 'their life is regimented' was detailed to read:

The doctor and his wife live in an established sub-
urb of Melbourne. Their house is quite large and is
always kept clean by the doctor's wife. The Scotch-
Guarded lounge suite and other modern furnishings
appear brand-new. The wall unit proudly displays
polished glasses and fine silver. The garden has been
carefully planned with flowers growing along the
brick walls and trees standing ten metres away from
each other. Hidden in the bookshelf amongst the
reference materials is the wedding album, never
opened but dusted every Wednesday.

The women found such models useful as they attempted
to locate the details behind their own generalisations. To
help them, we asked specific questions to spatialise the scene.
Who was there? What did they look like? What were they
wearing? Thinking? Feeling? Saying? What might the scene
look like to an outside observer watching? The questions
were, of course, more specific to the scene emerging for each
woman but the impact of the exercise can be illustrated by
my interaction with Helen.

Helen lacked confidence as a writer and believed her
domestic scenes were not worthy of writing. She agreed to
conference her very brief text in the presence of the group
and I tape-recorded our conversation to demonstrate how she
and other women might use everyday details to expand text.
We focused on a Sunday drive Heather had taken with her
family many years before and the events leading up to it. The
general statement in her text read, *'The Sunday drive was
disappointing,'* and I questioned her to elaborate the scene.
The following week I used our tape-recorded dialogue to reconstruct a first-person, present-tense monologue which I
presented to Helen and the group. Although this written text
was clearly scaffolded by my questions, I attempted to stay
as close as possible to the language Helen used.

It's Sunday. We plan to go out for a Sunday drive.
I'm getting the lunch for my family: a boiled egg for
the youngest Trevor, a salad sandwich for my hus-

band and daughter Judith, spaghetti for James. I'm having a salad sandwich as well, although it doesn't matter much as I'm happy to eat what's left.

We're all at the table, Trevor is in his high chair. We're talking about what's going on in the neighbourhood, but I'm the last to sit down as I'm buttering bread, toasting bread for the spaghetti, cutting vegetables, helping feed Trevor. When the family is finished they leave me at the table and leave their dishes on the table. The children have to have their faces washed, the dishes have to be cleared and washed. Then I can begin to get ready. Dad's getting ready, bathing the eldest child. I have to bathe the other two, but I'm not going out until the dishes are wiped up, the children are clean and fed.

When at last I'm done, I feel beautiful and ready for a relaxed drive with my family. I've finished my chores, have a nice pair of slacks and a clean blouse on and I've made up my face. I get in the car and we set off. Everything is done and I feel released from the house.

Then the children start fighting in the back seat. I take little notice, they're just children. Let them go. But Allan reprimands them and turns to me. 'I'm driving, why don't you look after the kids.' That's the end of my peaceful day. I'm put down and I'm shattered. I will pretend I'm not put off even though the tension is so great. I'll be silent for a while and then I'll pretend that everything is fine and I'll attend to the children and smile.

This text had a powerful effect on Helen and the group. Discussion focused on similar experiences shared by other women in the group, being silenced by partners and adopting that silence as their own. They were struck by the fact that detail made it possible to write, and write endlessly, as every potential statement had a meaning which could be further detailed. We also discussed the idea of selection and the difficulty of choosing the appropriate details. Proliferation of detail is not a good in itself and selection depends on the purpose to be achieved. In order to select, though, it is sometimes important to overwrite, to get the details out. Selections can then be made with profoundly different effects on the textual representation.

It is important to stress, however, that such detailing strategies leave their traces not only on paper but on the body and mind of the writer. If, following Kress (1996), we regard 'telling facts' as a design for subjectivity, what kind of subjectivity production is being encouraged? What might be the effect of this textual remaking on the writer Helen's subjectivity?

Firstly, it creates a text (rather than a blank sheet) and this is not to be underestimated. It validates aspects of Helen's domestic experience as significant enough to give body to a text that others respond to, and so constructs a positioning for her as writer. Secondly, it shows that the everyday, the ordinary can be crafted into an object which is *not* the truth but which represents a moment, a set of positionings. In Helen's text this involves a detailing of the woman's place as an extraordinarily complex mediation between the energy in the front seat and the back seat. It makes visible both her labour in preparing for a day off and the subsequent silence which shatters the day and the woman. Lastly, the writing disrupts discourses of the good wife and makes visible a set of contradictory and painful positionings that are not simply Helen's fault—but relate to larger discursive practices of marriage and generation which shape her experience.

Stories such as those written by Helen and Bella are important sites of cultural production. There are moments in the reproduction of dominant cultural narratives when intervention is possible, when such narratives are vulnerable to interruption if women can see the ways in which they are positioned by dominant discourses. For Helen, the writing increased both her confidence and her text production. In subsequent weeks she began to write prolifically in ways that continued to surprise her. She learned that it was possible for her to write, and that other women related to what she had to say, making available to her further opportunities for rewriting both text and self.

WRITING AS A POLITICAL PROJECT

While this description of strategies gives a sense of how we shifted the focus from issues of authenticity, emotion and true feelings to issues of power and representation, what it overlooks is perhaps the most crucial component of our working together: our commitment to a set of political purposes that encompass the individual but extend beyond her. It was this perhaps more than anything we did that allowed us to create distance between the writer and her text, especially when the experiences being written about were highly emotional and central to the writer's life purposes.

Our political purposes were feminist and transformative, and we were explicit about these. As workshop leaders, we took seriously the fact that there are few cultural storylines available outside dominant narratives of lost youth and physical deterioration. We regarded the women's stories as political and the writing workshop as a site for a politics of representation, where older women's stories could sit alongside and challenge dominant representations. Our aim was also to teach the women strategies to craft their writing, but such purposes were always framed within larger social purposes.

It is not new to highlight the importance of setting real purposes for writing. Early writing theorists such as Moffett (1968) in the United States and Britton *et al* (1975) in the United Kingdom argued for a school writing curriculum connected to writers' needs and purposes. This agenda was taken up by process writing advocates such as Graves (1983) who made real purposes and real audiences central to the writing pedagogy he developed. While I am cautious about the dangers of equating 'real' with 'truthful' or with the writer's 'real self', the insistence that writing should be meaningful to the writer is important. The stories of ageing workshops, however, taught me the importance of relocating that individual meaning in broader cultural contexts.

Such contexts are often absent from adult or process writing workshops where language is treated as neutral or where the personal is used primarily as a motivation to lure students into learning to write and read. For us, it was crucial to have a social, cultural and political reference point outside the self in order to contextualise what seemed to be idiosyncratic in larger patterns of power. We did not ask the women to write about themselves as an end in itself, but rather to produce 'collective autobiography' (Davies 1994), to develop a collective understanding of the discursive processes that have shaped ageing women in their specificity and their difference. Such purposes were also central to Haug's (1987) poststructuralist and feminist methodology, where stories of women's sexuality and sexualisation were used as a force for political action.

Issues of power and powerlessness are central for older women who have become 'invisible' to their culture. We adopted the practice of foregrounding such questions in our discussions and developed an exercise where we asked women to write about a time when they felt both powerful and powerless. This framing allowed writer's such as Rowena to play with the personal/political interface and reconstruct her experience of taking her husband home to die as a *victory* of discourses of dignity over discourses of medicine.

I JUST WANT TO GO HOME! A STORY ABOUT FEELING POWERFUL OR

THE DAY WE MARCHED TO PETER'S TUNE... DAH, DAH A DUMPTY DEE

'If you go home Mr Brown, you'll be dead within six weeks.'

'I just want to go home!'

'Mr Brown, if you go home you won't have access to our life saving machines. You will be dead within six weeks.'

'I just want to go home!'

'If you go home, Mr. Brown, it may not be possible for you to be admitted to hospital. You will be dead within six weeks.'

Are my heart beats breaking the silence? What will happen if I burst into tears? What if Harvey caves in? He hung his head even lower.

'I just want to go home!!!'

Overnight the news of Harvey's decision must have reached some of his friends who were employed at the hospital. So, imagine the procession.

First, came HARVEY in a wheel chair,
then a couple of social workers,
after them a wardsman, walking beside a nursing
aide,
next came a doctor in his white coat
An occupational therapist joined in and soon
after
a physio student,
And I was trailing the rear,
HUMMING

A DAH, DAH A DUMPTY DEE, A DUMPTY DUMPTY DUMPTY DEE, A DAH DUMPTY DAH, DUMPTY DEE . . .

DAH DAH A DUMPTY DEE, Harvey's coming home with me!

For one whole month we will be free . . . A DAH DUMPTY DAH DUMPTY DEE . . .

But what if he had said 'I don't want to die, let me stay in hospital,' what then?

DAH, DAH, A DUMPTY DEE!! HARVEY'S COMING HOME WITH ME!! A DAH DUMPTY DAH.

Rowena's text is poignant. The staging, the procession out of the hospital, the use of song as triumphal march work powerfully as a dramatic construct, as a social critique of the politics of death and dying. The genre of the children's story is invoked, as the procession of storybook-like characters—the social worker, the nursing aide, the occupational therapist—march out of the hospital with Harvey leading the way. This playfulness undercuts the fact that within weeks Rowena will be a widow and face the loss of her life partner.

Her personal pain and fear are always there—but understated—distanced. This is a time when Rowena felt powerful. She and her husband have asserted their rights over the hospital hierarchy, yet her grief sits at the edges ('But what

if he had said, "I don't want to die, let me stay in hospital" ')
as she carefully relocates the personal for purposes of social
critique. While many women did not take as overtly a
politicised stance as Rowena, they did use the representational resources of the workshop (conversations, critiques,
other women's writing) to disrupt cultural common sense
and build a politics of their own.

Their engagement in a rigorous intellectual community,
in critical processes of writing, talking, rewriting, positioned
them as powerful agents of their own representation and
fostered the production of counternarratives of older women's
sexuality, courtship, solitude, family relationships and experiences of death. Their stories have a great deal to teach a
culture that reveres youth and fears death. They pose important challenges to a public policy tradition which tends to
regard older women as a homogeneous group and image them
as passive recipients of government services, while older
women construct themselves as lively contributors to their
communities.

In 1999, participants in our longitudinal workshop groups
took a more active stance in the politics of representation by
performing their stories in the public arena outside the workshop. 1999 was the United Nations' International Year of the
Older Person and the women worked with a professional
director and scriptwriter to select, script and perform their
stories (Stories of Ageing Project 1999) for friends, family and
the wider community. As workshop leaders and researchers,
we had been committed to making public as many of the
women's stories as possible through our conference and journal publication across a variety of disciplines, including sociology, education, cultural studies, English, women's studies,
gerontology and social medicine. This was the first time,
however, that the older women directly took up a similar
discursive position and ventured to perform their narratives—
their bodies/texts/minds—for wider public consumption.

The women not only had a wealth of experiences to reflect
on, but a unique perspective from which to write and perform. They are not necessarily more confident than younger
writers, but their location in the life span means they have

a greater portion of the whole picture. They have lived longer, they have survived more and know how to live with both joy and disappointment. If their life is a map, more of the terrain is visible, the distance signposted and the letters readable without one's glasses. Meeting together in the workshops they found a community of survivors, a space of friendship and laughter. To do this narrative work at the end of their lives made a difference—to the older women and to those of us who were fortunate enough to work with them.

This chapter suggests that as teachers of writing we may need to develop greater self-consciousness about how narratives are made and how they might be written differently. If new narratives are ever to enter the culture, and women's lives, we need to explore the possibilities of counternarrative work. Without it none of us has any way of gaining enough distance to make dominant discourses visible and thereby to imagine alternatives. And most educational and policy contexts are badly in need of new stories and real alternatives.

Chapter Four

Who Said Argumentative Writing Isn't Personal?

❖

While chapter 3 relocates a number of process writing strategies within broader social and cultural contexts, this chapter argues for a rewriting of genre pedagogy, in particular the binary division between argumentative writing and personal writing and the notion that disenfranchised writers can gain access to power by being taught the prestigious genres of their culture. I make such arguments through a case study of a high school writer named Sasha and my attempts to teach her to write argument. I also develop a more explicitly linguistic approach to text development than in other chapters, while foregrounding the importance of teaching a poststructuralist metalanguage alongside the linguistic.

Sasha was a year 11 student who attended a large metropolitan high school in Melbourne, Australia. Her parents were acquaintances of mine who had asked if I could help Sasha with her writing. They feared that if she didn't get help soon, she would fail English. Sasha's struggle as a writer challenges narrow ways of looking at argumentative writing as 'not personal' and demonstrates that even when students are learning to write so-called 'factual' genres, complex questions of identity, authority and representation are involved.

On my first meeting with Sasha I was struck particularly by the way failure seemed deeply written into her body. As she sat at my dining room table, shoulders hunched forward, head inclined downwards, she seemed embarrassed at direct eye contact and gestured awkwardly at the pile of English papers she had brought to show me. This collection of red-penned essays was covered with D's and E's and a consistently negative commentary: 'expression is weak', 'no logical structure to the piece', 'no awareness of audience shown', 'not very informative', 'you need to enlarge upon the points introduced', 'you must produce more in the time allowed'. She was failing English. Sasha said her teacher was a bastard; he hated her she was sure. Could I help her?

I hoped I could as her pain and embarrassment were palpable. It is not comfortable being labelled stupid, believing you are and daily gaining confirmation in writing that this is the case. The demands of Sasha's year 11 and 12 curriculum, part of a state-mandated Victorian Certificate of Education, required that she be competent at writing argument, and she clearly was not. This was evident in a text written early in year 11. The topic was the Holocaust revisionist David Irving and the controversy surrounding his proposed visit to Australia in 1993. Sasha had been asked to argue whether or not Irving should have been denied entry to Australia.

SHOULD HISTORIAN DAVID IRVING BE ALLOWED IN AUSTRALIA?

The historian David Irving argues that the Jewish Holocaust is exaggerated, he is not saying it didn't happen he is just saying that people have added that all the people who died in the gas chambers, were not all Jews, in fact, he states only very few of them where Jews. His statements and allegations cause some people frustration and confusion. As well, the Foreign Affairs Department has refused the right for David Irving to come into Australia. The reason given are that it may offend some people who are still mourning their losses, and also it might begin protest. The decision to refuse entry to David Irving is based on keeping the peace.

A member of the Australian civil liberties union, John Bennett implies that it is wrong not to let

David Irving into Australia, because Australia is a
free country and freedom of speech is a right. Mr.
Bennett, has chaired two meetings for Mr Irving in
1986 and 1987, and says that his lectures were well
attended, and there was no protesting against his
beliefs, nor was there any racial tension or provoca-
tive violence.

On the other-hand Gareth Evans, the Foreign
Affairs Minister disagrees with John Bennett, believing that it is an unsuitable time for Mr Irving to
come, because of the elections, and also seeing that
people are very moody around this time. Furthermore Gareth Evans states that David Irving's views
are 'morally repugnant' and are not based on facts,
and since his last visit he has become more 'offensive'. The Foreign Affairs Minister believes that this
will only cause problems in Australia which is not
really needed, and may cause a 'breach of the peace'.

It is interesting to note that the print-media has
published articles on both sides of this question. It
seems to be a matter of freedom of speech versus
potential violence unrest and breaches of peace. The
government of the time is obliged to protect all
inhabitants of Australia hence its decision to refuse
entry to David Irving.

The most notable feature of Sasha's text is that it poses a
question she never answers. She doesn't, in fact, construct an
argument about David Irving, but rather summarises the ideas
of a variety of male experts and puts them together paragraph
by paragraph: (1) David Irving, (2) John Bennett, (3) Gareth
Evans. Paragraph four highlights the media viewpoint with
some oblique reference to her own position ('the government
is obliged . . . hence its decision'). The text bears traces of the
articles she has read and a few phrases she has learned are
appropriate to factual genres ('it is interesting to note', 'on
the other hand', 'hence'), although she does not necessarily
use these appropriately. For the most part, however, she ex-
cludes her point of view entirely from the text.

Her teacher's written response was brief and predictably
negative. 'D+ Expression—punctuation, spelling, sentence

structure. What is your view?' His focus is on surface features and Sasha's lack of attention to convention. His only genre-specific comment, 'What is your view', is misleading as it could be read to mean that Sasha's text will be improved with the addition of one sentence stating the writer's point of view. The teacher's failure to comment more usefully on what Sasha might actually *do* to construct argument is clearly problematic and dependent on the reading frames available to him.

Rather than target the teacher for criticism, however, I would ask how a critical writing pedagogy might equip teachers to deal with the complex issues embodied by Sasha's text? In Australia, genre theorists would argue that Sasha needs to be explicitly taught the conventions and linguistic patterns of argument in order to achieve success. Eggins *et al* (1987), for example, have argued that we need to teach students the 'genres of power' in order to empower them. Power is seen as a matter of access, where teachers make explicit the linguistic and structural features of genre in order to give students conscious control over powerful forms of writing. In doing so, it is argued, we can 'directly inculcate power' (Luke 1994) in those individuals who have not previously had power, and thereby achieve social change and mobility.

In this chapter I question the naïveté of such assertions, in particular the notion that an individual's life can be changed simply by being taught the 'prestigious' genres of her culture. Certainly, it was clear from the moment I met Sasha that all the genres in the world were not going to give her power unless she could also develop an authoritative and critical position from which to speak. She needed access to other discourses that could make explicit the relations of power which operated to construct her failure. As I considered how I would work with her, I had to take account of the processes by which she had acquired a failing student habitus (Bourdieu 1990)—the ways of talking, acting and moving, the ways of constructing reality and social relations, which marked her as different, as failure—and imagine how to rewrite these. I asked how is it possible to assert the authority required of argument when one is positioned as an inadequate, failing female student?

RELOCATING ARGUMENT

It has become common in school contexts to think of certain kinds of writing as personal and others as impersonal or factual. Usually the distinction rests on the subject matter, on whether or not the writer is representing aspects of her personal experience in text. If, however, we focus on the writer's subjectivity as well as the text, as argued in chapter 2, on who it is that is writing, on how they represent themselves in writing and the conflicts they face as they struggle with constraints imposed by conventions (Clark and Ivanic 1997:134), then it is difficult to think of argumentative writing as not personal or as separable from the writer's identity.

Certainly, my work with Sasha suggests that argumentative writing is no less constitutive of the writer's subjectivity than writing which explicitly focuses on the writer's personal experience. All writing is personal to the extent that it involves writers with gendered, classed, racialised, sexed histories negotiating and engaging with sets of equally gendered, classed, racialised, sexed discourses and genre conventions. To relocate the personal in this context means relocating an understanding of argumentative writing as *not* objective, impersonal and rational simply because it bears few textual traces of the person.

While Clark and Ivanic (1997) argue that American models of the writing process (eg, Hayes and Flower 1980, 1983) do not adequately represent aspects of writer identity as interacting with more cognitive concerns, such as formulating ideas, I would make a similar critique of Australian genre pedagogy. In rewriting that pedagogy, I pay greater attention to the interpersonal—to the power relations that shape the writer as she attempts to speak out in the genres her culture requires she adopt—and to disrupting the binary division between personal and factual writing.

Throughout the work of Sydney-based genre theorists, a clear distinction is made between genres that are personal—such as recount, narrative, moral tales, myths—and those that are factual, such as procedure, description, report, explanation and argument. In the early 1980s, genre theorists

Martin and Rothery (1980, 1981) produced a description and classification of genres using a corpus of texts written by primary school children. Subsequent descriptions of genres were developed according to grammatical and structural regularities in subject disciplines of geography, history, science and mathematics (eg, Eggins *et al.* 1987) and as resource materials for teachers (eg, Derewianka 1990; Christie *et al* 1990) with more discursive accounts produced by Christie (1990) and Halliday and Martin (1993).

Historically, this development of a typology of genres has been useful in confirming 'the dominance of certain text forms which students are required to write in both primary and secondary classrooms and across subject areas' (Richardson 1991:7). It also provided a framework for a sustained critique of process writing classrooms in the 1980s. Process approaches were critiqued, amongst other things, for focusing too heavily on personal genres, while factual genres, which were seen as providing students with access to the means for learning, were ignored.

One outcome of such reasoning has been to valorise factual genres as more objective, significant, prestigious (see Martin 1985) and to ascribe to them the authority to empower those who master them. This is exemplified by Derewianka's (1990) advice to teachers in a popular monograph, where factual genres cluster around terms such as *rational, intellect, logic* and *evidence* and are set in opposition to terms such as *emotion, intuition, feelings* or *prejudice,* which are seen to characterise the personal.

Such instantiations of the personal/factual dualism, however, are not just the province of Australian genre pedagogy. Kramer-Dahl (1996) examines a number of practices in North American basic writing courses and college composition where students are often encouraged to first write narratives of personal experience and then move to essays and arguments where they take a more reasoned, less emotional public stance. Through such practices a binary opposition between personal and argumentative writing is cemented; where private and public, emotion and reason, become the criteria which distinguish these forms of writing. One problem with such criteria, of course, is that they are not neutral. One term is inevitably privileged over the other as more valuable, more powerful, more male, and particular meanings of what is personal (emotional, private, secret) get associated as less powerful, as female.

While genre approaches would appear to valorise the argument side of the binary, some feminist pedagogues in women's studies and composition have reversed the binary and valorised the personal (see chapter 6 for a more extensive discussion). They have critiqued genres like argument as patriarchal, masculinist and excluding of women; in some instances they have rejected argument altogether 'on the grounds that it is a kind of violence, an instrument specific to patriarchal discourse and unsuitable for women trying to reshape thought and experience by changing forms of language' (Jarratt 1991:106). In her exploration of the intersections between feminism and composition, Jarratt (1991) argues instead for a rhetorical model of composition, based in political conflict, negotiation and attention to argument.

My own focus on the personal here should not be misconstrued as either rejecting the use of argument or claiming a moral superiority for autobiographical text. My argument, however, is that *why* and *how* students write is not separable from their lives. We need, therefore, to attend closely to issues of identity, regardless of the genre being constructed. Rather than reject the teaching of argument, I would rewrite the personal/rational binary opposition which informs it.

Foucault's explication of self-writing in chapter 2 disrupts this binary by extending the terrain of the personal and identifying a wide variety of material located in the public domain as available to the writer for making the self. Chapter 6 explores ways to disrupt the gendered nature of academic writing conventions and the subjectivities they construct. Clark and Ivanic (1997) also propose a politics of writing that explores the impact of particular discourse and genre convention on writer identity.

There are two moves to their argument. Firstly, they acknowledge that all genres are not equal but have privileged positions at particular historical movements. Because these patterns are seen to be in a state of flux and not fixed, they are also represented as malleable and not as constraining as is sometimes suggested by Australian-based genre pedagogy.

Secondly, Clark and Ivanic acknowledge that when writers experience strong pressure to conform to genres and conventions, they are also being positioned to adopt the interests, values and beliefs encoded in them. They argue that 'with more critical awareness, people might want to question and resist being appropriated by the dominant and statusful conventions, and thereby disassociate themselves from the interests, values, beliefs and power relations they represent' (Clark and Ivanic 1997:139). Equally, I would argue, they may choose to conform for any number of good reasons, including their life histories, affiliations to particular groups and/or pressure to succeed in particular institutional contexts. Such a conception, however, gives greater agency to writers learning genres such as argument.

When students like Sasha attempt to inhabit subject positions they do not feel comfortable with, this can become as much a focus of discussion as the content of their argument. If self-presentation in text is not seen as unitary or 'who the writer really is,' a more playful stance can be taken to manipulate subject positions in writing with the same attention teachers presently give to the 'logical' content of the argument itself.

In my work with Sasha I take up such a stance by regarding the teaching of argument as a design for both text and subjectivity—for altering a set of subject positions that kept Sasha feeling weak and inadequate. Sasha's ability to take a stand and put forward a viewpoint with strength and clarity involved not only a rhetorical stance but a life stance. The materiality of these texts, in turn, have recursive effects on the body/mind of the writer. While such issues are often more visible with writers who find academic writing difficult, they also apply to other writers in a wide variety of contexts.

In the remainder of this chapter I describe a number of strategies that I devised for working simultaneously with Sasha's inability to speak authoritively and her need to learn techniques for crafting argument. I conceptualise our work together as a material working on the body of a text and the body of a student. This involves a spatialised sense of the teacher working with the student on the page, and a spatialised sense of the writer's body experiencing discomfort in the writing, in trying to squeeze other people's knowledges onto the page and mould these into a coherent argument. These strategies can be separated into three components, but it was always the case that they worked recursively rather than sequentially:

1. developing a poststructuralist metalanguage to reposition the writer,
2. developing a spatialised metalanguage for structuring argument.
3. developing a linguistic metalanguage for building authority in text.

TEACHING CRITIQUE:
A POSTSTRUCTURALIST METALANGUAGE

> Rereading depends on being able to read all texts as makings, constructions, stories, which therefore have no epistemological authority other than as stories, and thus can be rewritten from another perspective, with a new setting, a different plot, a different hero, another ending. (Threadgold 1993:7)

Although Sasha was a writer who had little control of the recognisable patterning associated with argument, she was also a 16-year-old girl who felt harassed by her male teacher. She was located within a series of binary oppositions she was unaware of and had no control over: uneducated to her teacher's educated, failure to his success, female to his male, weak to his strong. As a consequence, I understood her failure to produce argument as, in part, a failure to believe she had an opinion worth hearing.

What Sasha needed was a map, something that would help her read her failure differently—as produced, rather than natural. I saw my job in part, as teaching her a metalanguage which would enable her to analyse her positioning and find new positions from which to speak. The metalanguage of poststructuralist theories is 'intentionally not linguistic' (Threadgold 1997:58) but can make explicit

> the ways in which teachers and students are caught up in multiple discourses, positioned in multiple ways—sometimes as speaking subjects mobilising the discourses through which they have been subjected/made subjects to powerful and liberatory ends, at other times in ways that deprive them of choice and of the possibility of acting in powerful ways. (Davies 1994:76)

Regarding Sasha's subjectivity as 'precarious, contradictory and in process' (Wheedon 1987:33), I worked to effect change in her mind and body. My own positioning in this relation was privileged as I worked with Sasha in the quiet of my dining room, free from the demands of thirty other students (in chapter 5 I demonstrate similar strategies with larger classes of high school students). Sasha's positioning was also privileged as a white, middle-class girl with parents who had the cultural capital to find her help outside of school. While it is commonly accepted that white middle-class children succeed in school settings because of a congruence between home/school values, meanings and practices (Clark and Ivanic 1997:121), Sasha's life as a learner was also enmeshed in a troubled history of gendered power relations which worked against class privilege.

Over time we developed a variety of ways to help Sasha deconstruct her multiple positions as failure, schoolgirl, student of a male teacher she feared. One practice involved rereading her teacher's essay comments as text, rather than as fact or truth—as a construct that could be analysed and deconstructed. Clark and Ivanic (1997:233) suggest a similar strategy where teachers and students critically examine both an assignment and the feedback received in order to make visible the teacher's construction of what is acceptable and what is not. Their aim is to raise student consciousness about the nature of the discourse community in which students are working and the effects of existing dominant conventions and practices, so these may be questioned or at least understood.

While my aim was to help Sasha rewrite a number of bad school stories, I worked hard *not* to construct a blame-the-teacher text. On the contrary, by using poststructuralist understandings of language and subjectivity I attempted to shift the focus to the ways individuals, including Sasha's teacher, are positioned in and through discourse. Sasha blamed her teacher and saw him as the source of her problems. I tried to give her new discourses to shift her understanding of power 'from the dominant and monologic voice of the oppressor at the top of the hierarchy to a heteroglossia of multiple local and specific strategies and tactics' (Threadgold 1993:9).

I provided a metacommentary for Sasha which made explicit the positions being offered by her teacher. I demonstrated, for example, how her essay comments emphasised only what she had *not* done, for example:

- no logical structure to the place
- no awareness of the audience shown
- not very informative.

I then asked what action she was to take. How was she to improve her control of logic, audience, information? She said she didn't know. I asked if the comments told her what to do. She said no. I suggested she had been given no information to help her take action. We also examined the advice she had received:

- you need to enlarge upon the points introduced
- you must produce more in the time allowed

Again I asked how she was to act on this advice. Again she said she didn't know. My aim in asking such questions was to relocate her 'I don't know' as a textual practice in relation to a teacher text that provided minimal guidance. I made it clear I would show her what to do, teach her strategies to improve her writing.

At the same time I provided discourses to help her reimagine her relationship with her teacher as one where she had some agency and control. We discussed her options: transferring out of the class, seeing the English coordinator, discussing her problems at parent-teacher interviews and/or learning to cope and succeed. I pointed out this would take time and that she would see no results for some time, given her teacher's reputation as a hard marker of even his most able students.

I also engaged in storytelling of a different kind to disrupt her elision of failure in English with failed identity. I told stories with 'another ending' where she succeeded, received help and learned how to pass English. I stressed she was probably doing the best she could, and if she could have done better she would have. A whole history of teacher-response texts had highlighted what she hadn't done, and she had come to believe them. Simultaneously, I worked with her on structuring argument (details in the next section) and mobilising linguistic resources she had no idea existed.

A turning point occurred three months into working with Sasha. She arrived at my home with uncharacteristic energy and announced 'You'll be proud of me.' She told the story of having received yet another D in English that afternoon. But instead of crumpling her paper in disgust, she approached her teacher after class and said 'It's no surprise to you or me that I'm failing. I don't know what to do. I need your help'.

In that moment I knew I could begin to teach Sasha to write with the authority required of argument. Her wording is significant. Linguistically, she positions herself in relation to her teacher as less powerful, less knowledgeable, as one who requires help. He is constructed as the one with power and knowledge, the one who knows what to do. Crucially, however, she takes power by asserting her need and demanding assistance. She thematises (Halliday 1985) her self, making the *I* prominent in each clause: *I*'m failing, *I* don't know, *I* need. No longer invisible, she speaks and is now seen both linguistically and as embodied text. She does not, for example say 'You need to help me' thereby giving prominence to the *you*, her teacher; nor does she say 'You never help me'. Instead, she observes discourses of politeness and does not accuse. After three months of working together, she refuses discourses which have constituted her as a powerless victim and which she has taken up as her own. Instead, she asserts her right to pass and repositions her teacher as the one who can help her achieve this goal. She has, in short, begun to rewrite the story with 'a new setting, a different plot'.

The speaking was essential to her development as a writer and suggests the power of poststructuralist discourse to help her disrupt her embodied failure. Her progress was neither smooth nor even, but from this point on she could stop blaming her teacher, stop fantasising about escape from his class and instead figure out how to write the genres required to pass English. The genres would not in themselves give her power, but they would help her relocate a personal story of failure.

STRUCTURING ARGUMENT: A SPATIALISED METALANGUAGE

I took seriously Sasha's need to understand how to structure argument in text. I assumed it would not be sufficient to simply tell her how to do this as years of previous advice had failed. Instead, I attempted to spatialise my pedagogy and make it more tangible. My aim was to reposition Sasha as a textworker, someone who could work actively on the body of a text with intent to shape reader opinion.

In chapter 3 I refer to Murray's (1982a) metaphor of the workbench, where teacher and student meet as craftspersons to shape the text until it finds its form. Here I want to introduce a more self-conscious sense of the teacher's labour in that crafting. Rather than providing monologic margin notes or a running commentary on the sidelines or even a good display at the front of the classroom, the teacher works with student text as clay; taking it apart, putting it back together, cutting slabs, punching, moulding, starting again. My focus here is on spatialising ways of working with the macrostructure of argument—what Australian genre theorists refer to as schematic structure.

I want to be careful here to distinguish Australian work on genre, which draws on Halliday's systemic linguistic theory (1978, 1985; Halliday and Hasan 1989) and subsequent theorisations of genre (eg, Martin 1985, 1992) from genre scholarship in composition studies in North America.

> Although the North American work has grappled with many of the same issues, such as the notion of genre both as a form of social action (Miller 1984) and as discipline-specific and political (Slevin 1988, 1991), no substantial rapprochements have been made between it and the Australian linguistic work. Collections edited by Freedman and Medway (1995a, 1995b), which bring the various traditions into dialogue, are important developments in this regard. (Lee 1997a:414)

So too, is a recent paper by Freedman and Richardson (1998) which examines both the common ground and differences between the two traditions, highlighting in particular the research-based orientation of the North American work and its refusal to take up either a focus on text type or the reductive classroom prescriptions of the Australian Sydney school. My own concern about the formulaic tendencies of genre pedagogy was highlighted in the 'Girls into Concrete' story in chapter 1 and has led me to argue subsequently, that genre-based approaches to writing in Australia do not constitute a critical literacy (Kamler and Comber 1996).

My work with Sasha has nevertheless been influenced by my selective use of this work, in particular its notion of genre as a culturally specific set of social processes that recur in particular social situations; and as a text type characterised by a distinctive set of stages and linguistic features. My aim, however, in developing the notion of clay work, is to rewrite genre as a more malleable text structure and to develop a spatialised metalanguage that can guide progressive drafts as the argument finds its form.

When I work with writers such as Sasha, I often begin by asking if they know how to structure an essay. If they have any idea, they usually say 'first you have to write an introduction, then the body, then the conclusion'. If they are able to talk at the paragraph level, they say 'every paragraph needs to start with a topic sentence'. When I ask, 'What's a topic sentence?' invariably they say, 'I don't know'.

While this kind of tripartite division of the academic essay is common, it lacks specificity and does little to help students visualise how to go about making their argument. In a popular genre-based approach for teachers, Derewianka (1990:76) develops a more explicit description of the text organisation of argument, as follows:

> The beginning of an Argument usually consists of a
>
> ### statement of position [thesis statement]
>
> often accompanied by some background information about the issue in question. There may also be some broad foreshadowing *[preview]* of the line of argument to follow.
>
> To justify the position taken, the writer must now present the
>
> ### argument.
>
> Usually there is more than one point put forward in the argument, and each one should be supported by evidence (eg statistics, quotes), and possibly by examples. The points are carefully selected and developed and add weight to the argument. All points should relate directly back to the statement of position, and there are often internal links between the various points too. At some stage the writer may suggest some resolution of the issue.
>
> Finally, there is an attempt at
>
> ### summing up the position
>
> in the light of the argument presented, reaffirming the general issues under discussion and possibly calling for action. (Derewianka 1990:76)

Certainly this description provides specificity and foregrounds the kind of meaning being made in each segment of the tripartite structure. What it also does, however, is present a static structure. While Derewianka herself would argue against a prescriptive pedagogy, her representation allows teachers to construct genre as a checklist of features that occur in predictable sequences. A number of Australian theorists working from critical literacy perspectives have critiqued this tendency to treat genre as formulaic and hegemonic. Lee (1997a), for example, argues that predictable descriptions of genre very easily become prescriptive and work to endorse the official discourses of schooling without questioning them. As a consequence genre pedagogy is often 'locked into a reproductive project of discursive identity and stasis, without the possibility of metacommentary on the status of the representations it is purveying' (Lee 1997a:439). Threadgold (1994) argues similarly that when descriptions of genre are read uncritically, they promote conservative, masculinist forms of literate practice while continuing to exclude nonmainstream literate practice.

To counter these tendencies, I try to introduce some dynamism into the process of teaching argument, some way of acknowledging that specific contexts do produce regularities of meaning that writers like Sasha need to learn in order to satisfy examiners and those who assess student progress— but that these are not simply to be mastered and accepted uncritically. This is particularly important in the Australian examination-oriented Victorian Certificate of Education system in which Sasha labours as a student.

Unlike the United States, where externally assessed SAT tests, not explicitly tied to school curricula, are used to rank students across the country, university entry for Sasha is determined by a complex system of central examination and school-based assessment which is graded by her teachers according to criteria externally determined by the Victorian Board of Studies. Examinations require students to produce extended writing through essays in order to generate a rank order of candidates, and these essays provide a powerful basis for discriminating between candidates.

In her critique of this system, Farrell argues that '[c]onventions of examination writing privilege certain ways of being in the world, certain ways of relating with knowledge, and certain writing identities' (1998:10). Her analysis of the ways examiners read exam scripts in centralised examination systems suggests that what examiners seek are socially and culturally familiar patterns of writing. 'Examiners reward candidates who provide for them, in the way they structure their essay, a familiar reading position, a familiar way of reading relevance, coherence and logic' (Farrell 1998:14). Where the structure of an essay is not familiar, it is read as unstructured and marked down accordingly.

Certainly, the normalising power of the centralised examination and the need to perform adequately to attain university entry needs to be taken seriously when working with writers like Sasha. These demands (and the pressure to reproduce culturally specific, formulaic structures), however, should not be confused with the only way to write argument, nor should it be assumed that students are going to produce a coherent structure or appropriate subjectivity without engaging in guided 'hands-on' claywork.

To provide structure to this claywork I have used the metaphor of a tree to spatialise argumentative writing—a metaphor taught to me by a wise secondary English colleague, Katrina Ratner, sharing some of her ways of working. She taught me to make the metaphor as visual as possible by actually drawing the tree. First the *trunk*, the base that holds up the tree, which is compared to the contention, or thesis, the overall argument the writer is making.

From the trunk I draw a number of *branches*. These grow out of the trunk; they are organic to it, a branching out from the central contention. These are the writer's main arguments, the major three or four points that make up the contention. Branches are stated in general terms and can be thought of as reasons for why the contention is held. I point out that when teachers make ticks in the margin of a student essay, often they are looking for branches; the tick signifies they have found one.

I then draw a number of *leaves* on each of the branches. These are the specifics that go with each branch—the details, illustrations, quotes, statistics. I stress the organic nature of the relationship between branches and leaves, leaves and trunk, and suggest that commonly students write masses of leaves without branches. The details are given (the leaves) but they are free-floating, without any branch to be attached to. While the reader may be flooded with detail, they never know what the argument is because it remains implicit and unstated.

Having established an organic model that is easy to visualise, I then transform the tree into a paragraph schema (see Figure 1). It is important to stress that I oversimplify greatly in order to establish a sense of pattern, a sense of ordering that some students seem unable to grasp without explicit teaching. Later, as they gain strength, it is possible to fine-tune and move away from such formulaic representations.

The first paragraph is the trunk. Here the writer states her position unambigously. As the trunk will of necessity be longer than one sentence, I demonstrate how this might be developed. I choose a topic the student is familiar with and model the kind of background information and contextualising needed to set up the trunk.

I then show how branches and leaves are distributed in subsequent paragraphs. I emphasise that the first sentence of each paragraph, what teachers call a topic sentence, is what I am calling the branch, and that attached to the branch are the relevant and appropriate leaves. The next paragraph states a new branch, a new argument, and attached to it are the relevant leaves, and so on until the conclusion or summing up. Clearly oversimplified, yes, but there is impact in embodying the paragraph, in showing how the branch operates at the start of each paragraph as a signpost to the reader. I highlight the writer's agency as a guide who must direct the reader through the branches, while connecting those branches both to the trunk (the overall position) and to the leaves that elaborate it. I highlight as well the writer's rhetorical location as someone who needs to anticipate and imagine what those with a different perspective might argue and build a rebuttal into their branches.

The strength of spatialising the structure in this manner is that students seem able to remember it and teachers can use it to guide successive student drafts. I illustrate by showing how I used the tree metaphor with Sasha to rewrite a failed essay written early in the year 11 on the Australian flag.

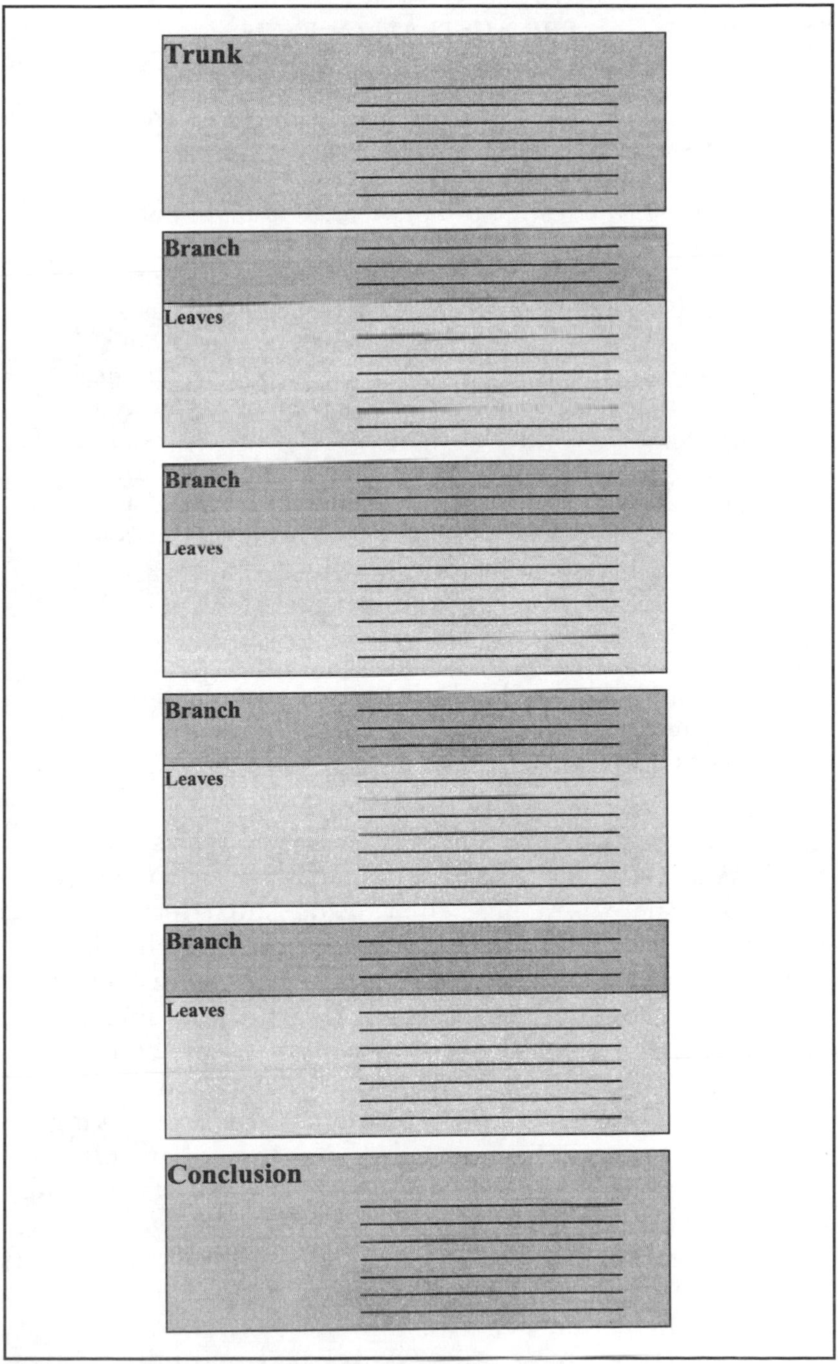

Figure 1. Tree Paragraph Schema

THE AUSTRALIAN FLAG

Last year the flag was being discussed by parliament, but this year it has been included in the issues for the election which makes the communities get involved.

It is interesting to note that 63% of 18 and 19 year olds say that they want to keep the flag as it is, and 72% of 50 year olds say to change the flag.

Considering that the flag has been with us for many years it represents our past and our connection with England, but we must also consider the fact that if Australia becomes a Republic, we need a flag to represent Australia not England. The only part on the flag that represents England is the Union Jack. The Union Jack represents the state of the Queen, but the Queen is not really ruler of Australia, so even more people resent the flag because it's not about Australia but about England.

As for myself, I am apathetic to this issue. I feel that there are more important issues to consider, but if I had to decide whether or not Australia should change its flag, I would have decided that they do need a new flag.

Using the tree structure, we can regard Sasha's first paragraph as a trunk and ask what is her position on the issue? It is clear there is none. When Sasha and I looked at the second paragraph and I asked where is the branch and what is the argument being made, it was clear there were only leaves but no branch. This analysis helped Sasha make sense of her teacher's comment in the margin (What conclusions do you draw from these percentages?) For the first time she could see he wasn't just being difficult, but was asking for the branch; as a reader he needed to know what point this leaf ('63% of 18 and 19 year olds . . . 72% of 50 year olds') was trying to support.

To the extent that Sasha asserts any opinion, this occurs in the final paragraph where her begrudgingly honest assertion of apathy is tacked onto the end ('as for myself, I am apathetic to this issue'). I suggested that structurally this was an advance on her earlier David Irving text, where she states no opinion and only compiles the opinions of others. My challenge was to teach her how to structure opinion into the trunk and at the start of each paragraph, in the branch position. We also discussed the problem of stating one's opinion too honestly in a centralised exam system which assesses that opinion for the purposes of university entry and of the need to sometimes create a fiction (Walkerdine 1990) in order to take a more culturally appropriate stance in text.

Rather than attempt repair work on this text (it clearly was not developed enough to do so) I asked Sasha to start again on the same topic. She would write a stronger argument on the flag, and I would scaffold her text using the tree structure. Her first effort at a new trunk was as follows:

> The Australian flag has been debated widely these past months of whether or not it should be changed. Some believe that the flag should be distinctively and uniquely Australian whilst others say don't change it, it represents our past.

Here Sasha shows there is conflicting opinion, even though she omits her own. I then rewrote the trunk, taking a very directive role in modeling and reshaping her words so she could see how a contention might be stated. I revised her first sentence

> Whether or not the Australian flag should be changed is an issue which has been widely debated these past months.

and asked her to write the next sentence where she states her opinion. After some discussion Sasha wrote:

> I personally feel that the Australian flag should be changed because I feel that it represents Britain too much when it really should be representing Australia and only Australia.

I explored with Sasha other ways of asserting opinion without using the personal pronoun *I*. In doing so, I was following the preference of her teacher who discouraged the use of *I* and preferred conventions where the self does not overtly intrude into the text. I experimented with deleting the *I phrases* from Sasha's sentence above ('I *personally feel that*,' '*because I feel that*') to demonstrate how she might cut out the pronoun and still assert a point of view. I also introduced phrases such as *it is important* or *it is clear* as alternate ways of adopting a more authoritative stance. Her revised trunk read:

> Whether or not the Australian flag should be changed is an issue which has been widely debated these past months. It is clear, however, that the Australian flag should be changed so that it represents an independent Australian Republic. A new flag will not destroy our relationship with Great Britain but rather more accurately reflect the current social, political and economic situation in Australia.

This was not a trunk Sasha could have produced alone, and the language bears the traces of my intervention. Yet it models what is possible, the kind of assertion she might aim for. I adopted a similar procedure in building subsequent paragraphs, starting with Sasha's approximation and modifying it, exploring alternatives, asking which sounded best, using the branch—leaf structure to guide our revisions. The branches in her final draft constructed a more defined argument than her earlier effort.

Branch 1 The current Australian flag does not represent Australia.

Branch 2 The flag must also be changed because it does not represent the current social and economic situation in Australia. The symbol of the Union Jack is offensive to Aboriginals whose culture and land were taken over by the British.

Branch 3 Historically, Australia has had strong bonds with Great Britain. Changing the flag will not change this fact.

The teaching interactions that scaffolded this text demonstrated to Sasha that language is malleable, like clay; that it can be reshaped until it does the job, and that there is often a struggle to get the structure right. Importantly, it showed Sasha that with help, she was capable of structuring argument with conviction, purpose and point of view. Once made, such texts work to further shape the writer's subjectivity.

CONSTRUCTING POWER IN TEXT:
A LINGUISTIC METALANGUAGE

As well as teaching Sasha a poststructural metalanguage and a metaphoric schema for structuring argument, I worked to develop linguistic resources to help her assert opinion. From my perspective, the most powerful application of systemic linguistics for teaching writing is Halliday's (1985) work on grammatical structure because it is an analytic tool which can be used by teachers in a variety of ways (Williams 1993). Here I discuss how I worked with Theme, Modality and Nominalisation to reposition Sasha as a more authoritative writer.

Theme analysis was particularly helpful to show how the writer's opinion can be structured into the clause. In a systemic functional grammar the clause is an important unit of analysis. The clause can be thought of as a message and the Theme as the 'element which serves as the point of departure of the message; it is that with which the clause is concerned' (Halliday 1985:38). In English, Theme comes first, it is what the clause is going to be about. For example, I can write either *On the weekend* we had thirty visitors or *We* had thirty visitors on the weekend. In the first example, *on the weekend* is Theme, in the second *we* is Theme. Each clause creates a different point of departure and foregrounds a different meaning.

I showed Sasha that Theme can be manipulated according to the writer's purpose and that different genres will produce quite different patterns of Theme. In a recount of personal experience, for example, it is the writer (*we*) who is often the focus as well as the sequence of events (*last weekend, and on Sunday*).

THEME

Last weekend	we went to Bali.
We	had a wonderful time snorkelling, swimming and surfing
and on Sunday	we saw Balinese puppets and dancing.
We	will certainly return there next year.

In an argument genre, by contrast, the focus is less often on the writer *(I)* and the fact that she has an opinion

| I personally | feel that the Australian flag should be changed |
| because I | feel that it represents Britain too much. |

and more on the ideas *(the Australian flag, it)* being argued

| | the Australian flag should be changed |
| because it | represents Britain too much. |

Theme analysis also gave us a tool for exploring the politics of writing argument, the fact that a Western cultural tradition places high value on analytic, logical thinking, on the development of arguments that are informed, supported, researched, impersonal (Derewianka 1990:78). In such a tradition the deletion of *I* is often read to signal greater objectivity and assertions of truth or fact. Whether or not Sasha ascribed to such values, it was important to explore with her the resources for not intruding self in text.

It was also important to show Sasha that other linguistic resources were available to soften and modify assertions of opinion, depending on the power relations operating. Modality is an aspect of grammar which expresses degrees of possibility, probability, usuality or obligation. There is a whole continuum of modality between absolute certainty and absolute uncertainty, between necessity and possibility and a variety of linguistic resources for expressing these, such as modal auxiliary verbs (eg, may, might, must, should, could, has to, can, ought); modal adverbs or adjuncts (eg, probably, possibly, obviously, definitely, occasionally); conditional clauses (eg, it appears that . . . , if the evidence suggests . . .); and hedges (eg, sort of, a bit, something).

In their discussion of the modality of writing, Clark and Ivanic (1997:132) point out that when a student writer constructs an identity as a member of an academic discourse community, it needs to be a suitably modest one where the status of the tutor-assessor-reader (as more knowledgeable) is not threatened. Furthermore, 'for student writers there is a fine line between sounding appropriately authoritative and overstepping the limits of their authority' (Clark and Ivanic 1997:156).

Where possible, Sasha and I played with the possibilities, using modality to soften (may, might, could) or strengthen (must, should) or exaggerate (absolutely, must, always) her developing assertions of opinion. The work was always done in the context of her texts (rather than as grammar exercises), taking them apart, treating them like clay, and aimed at helping her understand her own positioning as a high school writer wanting to be favourably assessed by her teacher and external examiners. In this way I strategically located the conventions of genre in a set of institutional power relations and created discursive space to ask questions about other language choices and their effects.

Perhaps the most powerful linguistic work we did, however, was on nominalisation (Halliday 1985). Nominalisation is the process by which verbs in text are changed to nouns (things) and information is packed more densely into nominal group structures. Writing tends to be more nominalised than speaking, and much of the content occurs as 'things' or nouns; in speaking, by contrast, the tendency is for much of the content to be coded as action and occur as 'process' or verbs. Sasha's writing, like that of many immature writers, was characterised by her use of the patterns of speech, and this also contributed to a less forceful way of asserting opinion.

I introduced Sasha to nominalisation when helping her write an introduction to a physical education essay. Her first draft shows many of the patterns of speech, where she encodes

the content in verbs (bold type), uses simple nominal groups
(eg, the sponsors, the media, the costs, the public, their personal sponsors) and no nominalisations.

> There **are** many reasons of why football **has grown**
> in Australia today. The sponsors which **stand** by
> their teams and **support** them. The media which
> you **would find** at every important match and the
> costs, of which **is** usually **covered** by either the
> public or their personal sponsors.

Sasha knew the paragraph didn't sound right but didn't know
how to improve it. Often when students are unhappy with
the immaturity of their writing, they run to the thesaurus
and try to fill their texts with large words. They believe that
increasing the complexity of their vocabulary will impress
teachers and examiners. Often, however, the problem is that
their writing is not nominalised, that it sounds more like
speech than writing. I explained this to Sasha and attempted
to illustrate by dividing her text into clauses.

A starting point is the student's ability to distinguish
verbs from nouns. Although Sasha was tentative in this
knowledge, she was able to identify the verbs in her introduction, and I helped her convert some of these into a more
nominalised form. We looked at each clause separately. I
showed her how 'The sponsors which stand by their teams
and support them' could be converted to a more nominalised
form 'the sponsorship of teams', whereby the action of *stand*
and *support* is converted to the noun form *sponsorship*. I
gave another example: 'The teams worked really well together'. I gave her the phrase 'the teams _____ ' and asked
her to supply a noun that could mean the same as *worked
well together*. She couldn't do it, so I supplied *cooperation*.
I showed her that the action could be converted into a noun
form, which freed her to now add another verb to the clause
and pack more information in, as in 'The team's cooperation
is great'. We moved back to her paragraph and worked through
each clause in a similar fashion and produced four nominali-

sations (in bold) in the following revision, reducing the number of words in her original introduction from 48 to 33, and the number of clauses from six to three.

> There are many reasons why football has grown in Australia and these include the **sponsorship** of teams, the **media coverage** of important matches, the **attractive lifestyle** of football players and **high financial returns**.

Teaching Sasha a simplified version of nominalisation and the linguistic metalanguage to talk about it, helped her produce a more concise, lexically dense text. She could not have done it alone and was dependent on my continuing interventions in her text. Simply telling students about nominalisation, however, does not help. I did not give Sasha a grammar lesson on nominalisation but instead used my linguistic understanding to identify her problem, explain it to her and demonstrate an alternative construction. I have documented here only one teaching interaction; there were many others over the period of the school year to establish the procedure as a strategic tool.

The aim, of course, was not nominalisation as a good in itself. Much has been written about the difficulties of overnominalised prose, its inaccessibility and stodginess. It seems to me, however, that too few students have anything approaching an explicit sense of the differences between spoken and written language, and this hampers them in their attempts to write argument. It is equally important to explore the ideological work achieved by nominalisation. Like the use of the passive voice, nominalisation allows for the omission of the agent. The conversion of verbs into nominals has the effect of putting the action in the background and not specifying the participants. In the sentence, 'The detonation of an atomic bomb in Hirsoshima resulted in widespread mortality', the nominalisations (*detonation, widespread mortality*) erase agency so that there are no identifiable people who drop the bomb or who die. These events just happen, and who is doing what to whom remains implicit.

While there may be various motivations for using nominalisation, for example, to make information more concise and highlight abstract ideas rather than people and actions (Hammond 1990), there are also ideological reasons for omitting agency and hence causality and responsibility. These purposes as well must be made explicit to students (Fairclough 1992) so that grammar is used not only to gain control of genres, but to make explicit the ways in which language operates to marginalise, exclude and disempower— a central purpose of a writing pedagogy which hopes to relocate the student as both a critical consumer and producer of text.

A HAPPY ENDING

The danger in telling any educational story lies in creating neat fictions of smooth progress without defeat. The work with Sasha was demanding, the progress slow. She often retreated to a position of 'I couldn't be bothered', especially when she continued to receive negative teacher response for a number of months after her progress was evident.

Yet there was a happy ending, exemplified by the opening two paragraphs of her final argument for year 11, where Sasha argues about the benefits of vegetarianism in an authoritative way that indicates a rewriting of both text and subjectivity.

VEGETARIANISM

Vegetarianism is not only morally right but healthy and ecologically wise. Young people today are becoming more aware about the foods they eat, but importantly they need to consider the values of vegetarianism. Considering the diets, where meat is obtained, people may not realise that, although it may taste good, meat is filled with excesses of fat, cholesterol and protein, whereas vegetarian foods are by far more healthy and do not require the slaughtering of animals. This way, you gain from the diet and nothing is harmed in the process.

Taking the life of another living species so people can eat it, is not only selfish but inhumane slaughter. It would be crazy to think of killing another human-being, so you could eat them. You would probably be sent to a psychiatric jail or institution for life. But who makes it right to kill an animal and eat it, then get away with it. Try understanding how people can take a life from this beautiful, natural world, and not even feel guilty for it.

In this text Sasha has moved a long way from either tacking her opinion onto the end or avoiding taking a position altogether. Her opening statement is assertive and she uses a variety of conjunctions to assert her reasoning (eg, 'not only . . . but,' 'but importantly'). While she has researched other people's ideas on vegetarianism, she uses these as evidence, as leaves connected to her branches. Unlike the earlier David Irving text, she no longer thematises the writer as the main source of ideas (*'John Bennett implies,'* *'Gareth Evans disagrees'*), but has yet to learn how to reference those ideas she does use. The text is more highly nominalised (*'the slaughtering of animals,'* *'inhumane slaughter'*) and uses more complex clauses in Theme position (*'Taking the life of another living species so people can eat it'*). Of course, there are still remnants of speech, particularly evident in the use of the personal pronoun *you* (eg, *'you gain from the diet'*) and emotional ploys (*'You would probably be sent to a psychiatric jail or institution for life'*).

Sasha received a B from her teacher for this essay and was ecstatic at the progress she had made. I have explored in detail a number of teaching interactions which were successful in producing both social and textual change—change in the way she viewed herself as a student and in her resources for producing argument. Her increased capacity to exert control over her writing and establish a presence within it was an embodied change which bears traces on her text and her person.

Part of the danger in exploring the complexity of learning to write argument through a case study of one student is the mistaken assumption it may give that such practices are reserved for the one-to-one exchange and cannot be implemented in classroom sites. In the next chapter I document the work of four teacher education students who engage in similar work with a much wider range of high school students writing argument for assessment.

CHAPTER FIVE

Critical Spaces for Learning to Teach Writing

❖

This chapter explores my work with four university students studying to become teachers. As in earlier chapters, I document the critical writing strategies I developed with these students, in particular the power of critical discourse analysis as an analytic frame for reading the personal. However, I also examine the problem of how to teach a critical writing pedagogy to students who are unlikely to have seen such a pedagogy in operation in elementary or secondary schools.

I regard such learning as risky for a number of reasons. First, because 'developing critical readers and writers of texts has,' as Lankshear (1994) points out, necessarily to do 'with enabling them to detect and handle the inherently ideological dimensions of literacy, and the role of literacy in enactments or productions of power' (1994:11). When teachers explore the networks of power that are sustained and brought into existence by writing practices, this 'means engaging with issues that are often controversial, certainly contemporary, and perhaps quite volatile' (Gilbert 1993b:324–5).

Second, because there are so few models to emulate. In Australia, where a great deal of innovative work has been done on critical literacy (eg, Muspratt *et al.* 1997), relatively little has focused on writing. In secondary contexts, critical reading practices have been documented (eg, Morgan 1992;

Mellor, *et al.* 1991; Janks 1993) including strategies of discourse critique, 'multiple reading . . . positions as . . . instructional strategy', and 'disciplined reading . . . "against the
grain" of a canonical textual corpus' (Freebody, Luke and
Gilbert 1991). In elementary contexts, analytic strategies have
been documented (eg, O'Brien 1994a; Comber and Simpson
1995; Comber and Kamler 1997; Knobel and Healy 1998) for
examining the ideological dimensions of text from the ear-
liest years of schooling. While a number of Australian journals devoted special issues to critical literacy in the 1990s
(eg, *Australian Journal of Language and Literacy* 1993 (16:4);
*Idiom, Journal of Victorian Association of Teachers of En-
glish* 1993 (29:2); *Open Letter, Australian Journal for Adult
Literacy Research and Practice* 1995 (6:1); *Interpretations,
Journal of the Western Australian Association of Teachers
of English* 1997 (30:1), few of these attend to questions of
writing.

Given this absence of scholarship on critical writing practices, I developed the writing workshop with my university
students as a site of collaborative research. My aim was to
position students as researchers of personal writing (their
own and others), as makers and critics of pedagogy rather
than consumers. I attempted to model a critical writing pedagogy in the university to help them imagine critical writing
practices in secondary schools.

My work with Karen, Tammi, Bronwyn, and David had
its beginnings in 1995 when they were enrolled in the first
of two literacy subjects offered in their Postgraduate Bach-
elor of Education degree. This degree is a two-year full-time
course designed to credential students as teachers of elementary and secondary school. The students who enrol have
completed a four-year undergraduate degree (often at other
universities) in a specialisation of their choice; for Karen and
Tammi this was English Literature, for Bronwyn, Music, and
for David, Sociology.

As part of the semester's work in this literacy subject, I
introduced Karen, Tammi, Bronwyn and David and their peers
to critical discourse analysis as well as genre and process
writing pedagogies. I was, at the time, in the early stages of
writing this book, and interested in working with a small

group on autobiographical writing. My success with older women in the stories of ageing workshops (see chapter 3) had made me courageous enough to work again with 'the personal' in the university classroom (the fateful site of the 'Till Death Do Us Part' story four years earlier). In a public announcement in a lecture, I invited interested students to participate, indicating we would apply discourse analytic tools, previously used with media texts, to their own writing and examine the consequences.

My work with the volunteering students, Karen, Tammi, Bronwyn and David, spanned eighteen months and can be divided into three distinct phases:

1. *September to October 1995.* For six weeks we read and critiqued one another's writing and experimented with how to use critical discourse analysis to read texts of personal experience.
2. *March to July 1996.* For six weeks, we continued to workshop students' writing and tease out implications for a secondary school pedagogy. Students then developed school-based units of work around concepts of power, representation and positioning. These were implemented to lesser and greater degrees during a five-week teaching practicum from June to July.
3. *August to December 1996.* Students worked collaboratively in pairs to reconceptualise and develop new units and implement these in 'safer spaces' during August and September. They analysed and wrote about their teaching, developed a presentation for the Australian Association for the Teaching of English Conference in September and subsequently developed that presentation into a videotaped lecture and a journal article, published the following year in *English in Australia* (Kamler *et al.* 1997).

CRITICAL DISCOURSE ANALYSIS:
A FRAME FOR RELOCATING EXPERIENCE

Our collaborative task was to teach ourselves (and later others) how to use critical discourse analysis to read texts of personal experience discursively rather than as expressions of our 'true inner selves'. Potentially, this seemed a powerful framework for making experience textual and thereby imagining other stories.

The term *critical discourse analysis* (Fairclough 1992, 1995) is used here to refer to an analytic approach to teaching and research that focuses on power relations in the institutional contexts of everyday life. While critical discourse analysis is marked by a fluidity of boundaries and a hybridity of analytic frameworks (see Kamler, *et al.* 1997, for a map of the territory occupied by critical discourse analysis in Australia and South Africa across a range of disciplinary fields), there is a common commitment by researchers and educators who use it, to a critically social rather than merely descriptive analysis. A key characteristic of the variety of approaches to critical discourse analysis is the way researchers move between broad social formations and microtextual analytic work (Luke 1995; Van Dijk 1993).

Discourse is a term used by both social theorists (eg, Foucault 1979) and linguists (eg, Kress 1985; Fairclough 1992). From a linguistic perspective, referring to language as discourse signals an intention to investigate it as a form of social practice. Discursive practice is manifested linguistically in the form of texts, using text in Halliday's (1985) sense to include both spoken and written language. We can analyse the features of text as traces or cues of the discourses operating, making the distinction here between text and discourse, central in Linda Brodkey's work. 'We read and write [and speak] texts, not discourses—at least my understanding of poststructural theory tells me to examine texts for traces of discourse or discourses' (Brodkey 1992:303).

As texts are always enmeshed within a range of social attitudes, values and assumptions about gender/class/race relations, an analysis of texts can make visible the discourses operating and the part they play in constructing subjectivities.

Of course, most poststructuralist work does not engage with theories of language or close textual analysis. My approach to critical discourse analysis, however, foregrounds intersections between systemic functional linguistics (Halliday 1985) and poststructuralist and feminist theories of the subject and discourse (see Kamler 1997 for a more extended discussion). Implicit in my decision to combine linguistic and poststructuralist frameworks is a critique of both traditions: of a Hallidayan linguistics, for its lack of an adequate social theory (Kress and Threadgold 1988; Lee 1993) to support the grammatical theory, and of a more general poststructuralist refusal to use linguistic and close textual analysis.

LINGUISTIC REFUSALS

My use of linguistics owes much to Halliday's systemic functional grammar, a material theory of language which rejects the Saussurean opposition between form and content—between language as system and language as practice. In theorising the relation between the textual and social, between the functions of language and the immediate contexts in which language is used, Halliday provides a metalanguage for relating the details of lexicogrammar through social interaction to social context.

Faigley sees the systemic functional linguistics developed by Halliday as a useful tool to investigate the cultural assumptions in 'unproblematic readings of everyday texts' (1994:91). In doing so he makes a crucial but not always understood distinction between American structuralism and European structuralism, in particular the tradition of critical linguistics (eg, Halliday 1978; Fowler and Kress 1979; Hodge and Kress 1988). While the former separates form and content and neutralises linguistics as an objective instrument of analysis, the latter uses linguistic analysis for the study of ideological processes which mediate relationships of power and control. Had the Hallidayan work been better known in the American context, Faigley argues, it might have influenced composition studies in the 1980s.

However, one of the limitations of most critical linguistics, as Faigley rightly points out, is that it does not contain a theory of social critique—an absence which leaves an imbalance of attention on the linguistic form. 'The tools of linguistic analysis can be useful in analyzing how subject positions are constructed in particular discourses. The notion of subjectivity itself, however, is far too complex to be "read off" from texts' (Faigley 1994:110).

While Faigley is unusual in the American context in exploring the potential of critical linguistics, he seems unaware that a number of theorists in Australia, also finding no adequate social theory to support the linguistics (Poynton 1985, 1990, 1993; Lee 1993; Kress 1985; Thibault 1991; Yell 1990; Threadgold 1997), have explicitly reworked the Hallidayan framework under the impact of poststructuralism, semiotics and/or feminism. Within such work, notions of embodiment, relations of power, discursively produced subjectivity and even habitus are not seen as incompatible with Halliday's construction.

The most interesting recent formulation has been produced by Threadgold (1997) to whom this discussion owes a great deal. Threadgold proposes a feminist poetics for the performance of a feminist critique, where the idea of grammar as corporeal trace offers many resources for a feminist analysis of the networks of textual practices that constitute genres, discourses and making meanings differently.

Of course, as Threadgold (1997:85) points out, most poststructuralist theorists have found linguistics and structuralism 'to be patriarchal (de Lauretis), to be objectifying science (Foucault), to have been guilty of the attempted colonisation (as metalanguage) of all other semiotic systems (de Lauretis, Eco)'. But the refusal of linguistics, she argues, is based on a very narrow reading of what linguistics might be—on certain traditions of American structural linguistics which reject the possibility that the basis of language is meaning and that meaning is socially constructed.

There is also confusion, Threadgold argues, over what a linguistic metalanguage (a language to talk about language and semiosis) is, between grammar and what Halliday calls a grammatics, that is, between language itself and the linguist's metalanguage. In an argument too complex to rehearse here, Threadgold provocatively suggests that

> the metalanguage of a functional linguistics is no different to the metalanguage of Freudian or Lacanian psychoanalysis, the metalanguage of Marxism, the metalanguage of Foucauldian poststructuralism, or the emerging metalanguage of the archetypal refuser of metalanguages, deconstruction (the *trace*, the *arche*, the *pharmakon*, *différance*, *destinnerance*, the *signature*—one could go on). Linguistic theories, *qua* grammatics, cannot provide any 'objective means' of analysing texts. In using them as metalanguages, we are again, as in all other kinds of theoretical activity, doing what Greimas has characterised as 'making meanings by transforming meanings.' (Threadgold 1997:108)

While my decision to combine linguistic and poststructuralist frameworks then, is not unproblematic, it is a choice which I believe contributes positively to the development of a critical writing pedagogy. If we take up the Foucauldian notion that as members of a society we are constituted in and by the available discourses and that they speak through us (Janks 1997:338), it should be possible to analyse personal writing for discourses and subject positions. If we regard discourses as manifested in linguistic form in texts, we can examine the specificity of linguistic choices as traces or cues of the discourses operating. This provides a political context and a way to theorise the construction of 'personal experience' in relation to the broader sociopolitical context of power relations.

One of the challenges of using critical discourse analysis on personal writing, however, is the difficulty of estranging oneself sufficiently to read experience as text.

> Looking at a text critically is not very difficult when we disagree with it—when the positions that it offers to us as readers are far removed from what we think and believe and value. In cases where we begin from

> a position of estrangement or alienation from the
> text it is easier to read against rather than with the
> text. The interests served by the text may be appar-
> ent; the reader may even be at the receiving end of
> the consequences entailed and might have little
> difficulty in questioning the text. (Janks 1997:330)

When one is the writer and her values and beliefs are deeply
entrenched in patterns of language use, such distance is more
difficult to achieve. A group of critical readers, however, can
play a crucial role in this regard, collectively estranging the
writer from her text.

While Tammi, Karen, Bronwyn and David were novices
at critical discourse analysis, they were well-positioned to
attempt this work. Compared with Sasha (see chapter 4) or
the older women (see chapter 3), their knowledge of both a
linguistic and poststructuralist metalanguage was far more
self-conscious and accessible as an object of inquiry itself. In
retrospect, the structuring of the writing workshop as a site
of research, where we would work together to explore the
power of critical discourse analysis and my evolving pedagogy, was significant in relocating students as innovators of
new practice rather than emulators of the old.

READING STUDENT WRITING CRITICALLY

From September to October 1995, I met weekly with Karen,
Tammi, Bronwyn and David to write and critically read their
writing. I initially set the task of writing about a significant
relationship in their lives. Although a potentially intrusive
topic for a group of 'strangers', it deliberately challenged the
boundaries of comfort and our willingness to allow 'the personal' to be critiqued.

As a starting point we used critical questions developed
in the 'stories of ageing' workshops (see chapter 3) to ask
questions about their texts. Often we examined a powerful
phrase or image and then moved to absences, to what the
writer had not said. We also attended closely to lexical selec-

tions or wordings and tried to read these as traces of the discourses operating. Often our attention was taken by phrases that overgeneralised or understated a situation. In one text, which explored a vexed relationship between cousins, we focused on the line

> As kids we got along well enough; we saw each
> other fairly often as we lived in the same area.

The phrase *well enough* was evocative for the group, occurring as it did amongst a catalogue of the cousin's annoying behaviours. *Well enough* signalled a refusal by the writer to overtly criticise, a commitment to such family fictions as 'everything's fine' and the need to 'keep up appearances'. This phrase lead the group in turn to examine discourses of family life more broadly and the embargo on revealing family secrets, as itself discursively produced. I was taken by the intense energy generated by this discussion and so set the phrase 'we got along well enough' as a topic for the following week. In this way I moved between written text and discussion to guide the writing in subsequent weeks.

One student examined the phrase 'well enough' as a device for keeping the family peace.

> Although I have no respect for Sam and I only tolerate him for Susan's sake, I '*get along well enough*' with him publicly. I don't expand on his faults to my sister, and I try to avoid the Sam-bashing sessions my dad occasionally draws us into. If I wasn't related by marriage to Sam, I wouldn't give him a second thought. I am though, so it's important to keep up appearances . . . It isn't my place to tell my sister who to love. No, the best answer for me is to keep 'getting along well enough' with Sam so that we can all live in relative peace.

Another student explored the stress of negotiating with her 'in–laws–to–be' and the silences implicit in this relationship.

Alison is not my mother, she is not my mother-in-law, she is not even my relative . . . she just acts as though she is.

She questions me about what I cooked her son for dinner last night and yet she sends us cakes and casseroles . . . we *get along well enough*.

She drops disparaging remarks about my bomb of a car and yet she lends me her Seca to drive . . . so we *get along well enough*.

She comments on my weight and watches what I eat and yet she gives me clothes that are too big for her . . . so we *get along well enough*.

She queries my financial stability and yet she is forgiving if the rent is late . . . so we *get along well enough*.

She patronises my wardrobe and yet seeks my approval of her new purchases . . . so we *get along well enough*.

She glances disapprovingly towards my hand on Peter's leg and yet suddenly becomes overly-demonstrative toward her husband . . . so we *get along well enough*.

She makes me feel inadequate and unsuccessful in my attempts to fit in with her social circle of patronising charity volunteers and yet these same friends share the many stories of Alison's praise for me . . .

So Alison and I, we *get along well enough*.

While Tammi, David, Bronwyn and Karen often wrote on the same topic, I also directed them to explore phrases and images particular to their own texts. One text, for example, explored the contradictory positions a '90's wife' occupies as she attempts to pursue her own goals as well as those of her partner. I suggested the writer might explore discourses of 'the good wife' in greater detail by comparing her mother's positioning with her own. An excerpt from her text gives a sense of the power of that metaphor for remaking both subjectivity and text.

The Good Wife never disagrees with her husband publicly. She is his biggest fan, quick to sing his praises and loan him her smile when he's feeling down. She disagrees with him in private sometimes, but without deflating his male ego, which must be boosted, not torn down. She wants her man to be strong, independent and ambitious, and these are not traits she sees as imperative for her personal development. She must be nurturing, she must have the strength to bear the weight of the family woes, she is the housekeeper of her man's soul. Whatever he does, no matter how outrageous or infuriating it may be, is not reflected on them as a good happy married couple, so long as she is virtuous . . .

I feel my role as the housekeeper of Simon's soul quite keenly. Unlike the situation with my parents, where Mom is virtuous and Dad frankly isn't, Simon is virtuous, just in need of a bit of 'soul cleaning' every now and again. He doesn't know how to vent like I do, so things get a little musty in there. Every once in a while, I come along with a down feather broom and non-abrasive cleaner, which I hand over to him while I sit and croon soft, comforting sounds. He vents and cleans out his insides, and I, the nurturing good wife, collect the nasties of his past to be disposed of elsewhere.

These texts generated intense pleasure as group members learned to read the discourses in each other's writing and provide more than an empathic response to texts of personal experience. Simultaneously, a metacommentary about the pedagogical implications of our work developed as students asked questions about our workshop practices. What difference did our critique make to the writing produced? What was the value of reading each other's work critically? Did it make a difference to subsequent writing? Did it influence revisions for the better? What social action (if any) could be taken as a consequence of our critical readings?

While there were no simple answers to these questions, they guided our work at university and in the secondary school the following year. At the end of our first six weeks working together, student evaluations stressed the material

effects of our critical writing practices on their personal and
professional lives.

> This has changed my writing dramatically. I now
> have the words to say what's been frustrating me
> for years. I can name the discourses now that be-
> fore, I'd think why am I feeling this. You know
> Simon [husband] was making me feel inadequate in
> some ways; he hadn't told me I was inadequate but
> I could feel it and I took it as personal, like what
> am I doing wrong. And then a lot of things have
> opened up and I listened to what he was saying and
> I heard the sexist discourse. Then he's sort of going
> 'you're gonna have to help me with this' because he
> recognises it's serious. I mean it's fantastic we both
> can name these things now, put them out there and
> quit making them this personal form of attack and
> deal with it as a social construction that we can
> deconstruct. And I mean my evaluation of this is
> that it's fantastic.

One student spoke positively of the writing creating a space
to make discourses visible and not simply be subject to them.

> Yeah it's confronting for sure, but it's a relief too
> because you see it for a social construction and you
> can say 'oh this is what just poured out of me' and
> you know I can say 'oh I know where that came
> from. It's not just she's a bad person and she's hor-
> rible for doing this. I can say oh this came from me
> and I can change it too. I don't have to stay like
> that.' Yeah actually, I don't feel like I'm being at-
> tacked so much as I've had my eyes opened.

For the one male member of the group, the experience of
reading sexist discourses was disturbing, but powerful.

> I found the strong feminist perspective from some
> members of the group challenging, enlightening and
> frustrating. Challenging because I thought I was

pretty much free of sexist belief and action. To be
made aware of the range of patriarchal discourses
running through society and then identifying some
of these elements in myself was an uncomfortable
realisation. To think that you're full of these
influences and that for a variety of reasons, you can
get away with it as a white male and so are possibly
part of one of the most insidious forms of sexism is
confronting. As is the prospect of change. Nobody
is immune to the abundance of discourses that shape
our society, but it is easier to identify them in other
people than in yourself.

Karen, Tammi, Bronwyn and David's texts and developing
discourse critique were crucial in pushing my own understandings as a teacher educator and literacy researcher. The
kind of collaboration we developed is unique in universities,
where undergraduate students are more often asked to evaluate preexisting bodies of knowledge than create new pedagogical interventions with their professors (unless they are
PhD students or have higher institutional status). The group's
writing and critique, however, were central to the development of my own theorised practice.

I was therefore delighted when they asked if we could
continue working the following year and explore more directly the implications of a critical writing pedagogy for secondary school contexts. Institutionally, I was able to locate
our work in 1996 as an assessable individualised project where
students had scope to designate an area of interest and find
an academic willing to supervise them. I became their 'lecturer'; they my 'officially enrolled' students.

RELOCATING STUDENT TEACHERS
AS WRITING RESEARCHERS

Education students occupy an uneasy space between two
discursive locations: as students in a university classroom
and as student teachers in a secondary school classroom. In
both sites they are object of the evaluative gaze; at university

their academic work is scrutinised for its strengths and weaknesses, for its control of particular disciplinary knowledges; at school their teaching practice is evaluated by supervising teachers against the criteria of 'good teaching' as it is currently practiced. There is notably little space, in either location, for innovation, for moving beyond the boundaries of what is already practiced; for being seen as young colleagues who might have something to teach as well as learn.

My aim, by contrast, was to create a pedagogical space that maximised collaboration, response and agency, a 'safe space' where young teachers could challenge dominant discourses of literacy teaching and implement alternatives. While I am not unaware of the irony of advocating a 'safe space' for a writing pedagogy which engages the politics of critique, it is nevertheless important that such spaces be created—discursively and materially—in universities and schools.

In assembling any pedagogy for literacy, teachers use local knowledge of their particular sites and draw on a range of theories (Kamler and Comber 1996). Student teachers are uniquely positioned in this regard, as their work mediates the space between the university and the classroom in specific and embodied ways which can disrupt the usual practice/ theory binary. This need not be a matter of learning 'theory' at university and then practicing it in the 'real world' (with all the disappointment this may entail), but rather engaging students in a theorised practice which helps them learn how to work outside dominant paradigms.

To this end I structured four writing assessment tasks as a framework for our work during 1996: a research paper on critical literacy, a school-based unit of critical literacy lessons, a conference paper based on these units and a journal article based on the conference presentation.

These tasks are clearly located within the discursive field of the university. I wanted students to read widely in the professional literature and develop classroom practices informed by current theorising and debates in the field. Students knew there were few models to emulate and that their school-based writing units would, of necessity, be experimental. By designing their teaching as research, however, and asking them to report their findings to a professional teaching community, students also experienced a shift in their student subjectivities. A research lens enhanced student authority by relocating their university work and teaching in the discursive field of English teaching, where students usually have low status as novice.

To make a conference paper and journal article compulsory created a discursive space where students were authorised to speak. Because these professional texts were prepared in the university, I could scaffold student performance and make explicit a number of conventions of the academic research community. When their journal article was accepted and they negotiated the editor's extensive demands for revision, the students were relocated as insiders to an educational community in which they are normally positioned as spectator, not participant.

Most teacher education students, by contrast, negotiate the complexities of learning to teach writing alone. They have university classes (where people like me explore writing pedagogy as theorised practice), and they have school teaching practice advice and support. Their struggle to learn to teach, however, is not collaborative in the sense of having a community to discuss and critique their evolving pedagogies. And writing rarely plays a significant part in this process.

When Bronwyn, Tammi, Karen and David returned to the university demoralised (after a five-week teaching practicum from June to July), we discovered that the classrooms where they tried to implement their school–based units were anything but safe. Together, we teased out at least two major kinds of difficulties. The first was due to their inexperience with how to make writing practices 'critical'.

Karen, for example, struggled with how to use linguistic analysis in a critical manner. She, of course, was not alone in her struggle as issues of linguistic imperialism and structuralist hegemony have been areas of intense debate in Australia (see, for example, Lee 1997a; Threadgold 1997) and the United States (see, for example, Faigley 1994 for a discussion of why a structuralist paradigm makes it impossible to accomplish critique). Here Karen reflects on the difficulties she faced as she tried to teach nominalisation to a group of thirty year-11 students in a coeducational state high school.

> In my initial lesson, the first obstacle I had to over-come was the students' lack of understanding of nouns and verbs. This was alleviated (so I naively thought at the time) by giving them a handout with information about clauses, parts of speech, and simplified definitions of nominal groups. In my second lesson, I introduced the students to the term 'nominalisation', gave some basic demonstrations on the technique of nominalising, handed out worksheets that carefully selected samples of sentences from their essays, and asked the students to identify the verbs and turn them into nouns. The scene that followed was one of confusion and despair as I vainly attempted to direct some students to 'spot the verb' and debated with others about the benefits of 'nominalising'. As they were struggling to get enough words down in the first instance, it was difficult for them to see the benefit of reducing the number of words by nominalising. Those students who were able to complete my nominalising tasks successfully were those who used it in their writing already.
>
> By focussing on the linguistic tools I lost sight of the fact that from a critical perspective, it is how the tool is used and what it is used for that is significant. I could no more improve their writing by teaching nominalisation than I could if I returned to a 'back to basics' approach. The experience revealed to me the dangers of technical explicitness becoming an end in itself and as such preventing teachers and students from asking the questions that need to be asked. (Kamler *et al.* 1997:31)

The second kind of difficulty was due to a misunderstanding about what students were trying to do because their work was perceived as dangerous. This was Tammi's experience when she attempted to work critically with the journal writing of thirty year-8 students in a prestigious private girls' school in Melbourne.

Tammi's unit aimed to develop critical understandings of how values are constructed in language. The linguistic dimension of her work explored differences between active and passive voice, the fact that active voice explicitly states who is doing what to whom (as in, the boy hit the girl) while passive voice often downplays or omits agency (as in, the girl was hit by the boy, or the girl was hit). To encourage such understandings, Tammi developed the following worksheet for students.

- choose 5 sentences from your journal
- underline the verb in each sentence and identify the tense
- label the subject and object in each sentence
- rewrite each sentence from the active to the passive voice (or vice versa) and discuss the effects on the meaning (Handout)

Such linguistic-based work was acceptable to the classroom teacher, and Tammi was given time to explore it over two lessons. Problems emerged, however, when she developed the following assignment, using linguistic understandings, to revise student's journal writing.

Write a story which is drawn from 3–5 entries from your journal. The story should be written in the third person and be at least 500 words, though it may be longer. It may be useful to imagine a frame around your story as though it is a picture, and ask yourself, does everything in the story fit in the picture? While you are writing the piece you should consider the following aspects of your writing:

- How do you portray your characters (yourself and family)?
- How do you resolve problems (not in real life but in the writing) and conclude the piece? Is it a strong clear ending?

- Are there contradictions in your portrayals? Do
  these make the story stronger or weaker?
- How do you use the passive voice to change the
  focus and relations of power?
- Is there enough description to give a complete
  picture? Have you used enough detail? (Handout)

Many students spend years writing journals because their
teachers believe a focus on the personal will motivate them
to write. Journals, in fact, are often regarded as the sacro-
sanct terrain of student voice, a space for 'truth' and real
feelings, not a space for critique. Tammi's challenge to year
8 students, to write about themselves in third person and
view their family and friends as characters in a story, created
the opportunity to look differently at 'reality' and imagine
the telling of other stories.

It also confronted a whole set of school values that idealise
the personal journal as 'honest', 'natural', 'genuine', 'real', 'spon-
taneous', 'sincere' (Gilbert 1989:24) and therefore not open to
critical appraisal. The school was concerned that student journals would be made the object of Tammi's analysis in her
conference and journal presentations. Despite assurances that
all textual selections would be anonymous and approved by
the school prior to publication, the school worried about the
dangers of putting private–school student lives under scrutiny
with all the attendant risks to parent and school reputations.

In the end, Tammi's unit was sidelined. When time ran
short, her lessons were postponed; the supervising teacher
decided the assignment could be written at home and that
Tammi could collect the texts after her teaching practice was
finished. Of course, without sufficient modelling, guidance
and dialogue to help students select and fictionalise their
journal entries, this critical writing activity had little chance
of success. When Tammi called twice to arrange to collect
the texts, she was told they were not yet available.

This resistance reminds us that a critical writing pedagogy may be seen as 'risky business' because it does not
simply treat language as neutral communication. While
schools are right to protect the lives of their students and
reject the journal as a space for confession, they might also

reflect on how their own practices encourage the voyeurism they eschew. It may well be that an assignment such as Tammi's, which relocates a common genre of schooling as an object of inquiry and examines its grammatical and ideological effects, has a greater chance of working against voyeurism and an unreflective stance on experience. As a student teacher in another teacher's space, however, Tammi was not given the opportunity to find out.

Following the practicum, I therefore provided space for Tammi, Karen, Bronwyn and David to examine their personal sense of 'failure' and relocate it as discursively produced in particular institutional and pedagogic relations. It was clear, however, that they also needed a second chance, a 'safer classroom space' where they could try again. They needed classroom teachers willing to let them experiment with critical literacy and/or engage the politics of reframing literacy curriculum.

The following discussion presents excerpts from Karen, Bronwyn and Tammi's descriptions of the pedagogies they devised in these 'safer spaces'. This text varies somewhat from the published description of their work (Kamler *et al* 1997) in wording and sequence, as it is based on essays written prior to publication which have been revised by the students for the purpose of this chapter. I therefore use italics, rather than quotation marks, to distinguish their writing from my own.

KAREN AND DAVID: THE VBOS TEXT REVISITED

Karen and David worked in a year 11 English class in a regional coeducational state school outside Melbourne, serving a middle to lower middle-class community. This was the same classroom where Karen had worked during teaching practicum. Her supervising teacher believed critical literacy had potential to help her year 12 students write a critical media analysis and argumentative essay, major assessment tasks in the Victorian Certificate of Education.

Karen's earlier struggle to use linguistic analysis in a critical manner found temporary resolution as she and David developed critical practices for teaching argument. Each year,

year 12 students receive written advice from the Examination Assessors about what constituted an A graded argumentative essay in that year's exam. This advice is taken seriously by schools as an attempt to make explicit the criteria for successful student performance. David and Karen, however, chose to make the advice itself the object of their critical inquiry (much as I did with Sasha's teacher's essay comments in chapter 4), rather than simply present these criteria as given. Karen writes:

This text seemed a good choice for introducing students to the notion of language as socially and culturally located as it had an obvious impact on their lives. Read as a 'text' the assessor's comments also highlighted a contradiction— that students were expected to write with power and authority in circumstances where they had little of either.

David and I took the assessor's comments into the classroom as a 'text' with the aim of making explicit to the students how power and authority can be constructed in writing. The excerpt we selected was as follows:

> *The students should avoid simply summarising what others have said about the issue, and concentrate on arguing through to a position. The writer's aim is not simply to advocate a position, but to attempt to draw readers into the argument, to influence them to share an informed point of view on the issue. (Victorian Board of Studies, 1995)*

The students reacted favourably to the idea of looking at advice from the Victorian Board of Studies from a perspective different to that which they normally experienced. As a class, we deconstructed the text using the following questions about the conditions of production and interpretation, based on those developed by Luke, O'Brien and Comber (1994):

- *Who produces the text?*
- *For whom is it produced?*
- *Why has the text been produced?*
- *What is the text trying to do?*

Through our discussion we built up images of the Victorian Board of Studies as an agent of power who develops the curriculum and decides how students will be graded; of teachers as mediators of that power, who guide students to produce VBOS approved texts; and of students as subject to both. While these questions made the ideological dimensions of text more explicit, we further explored questions of reader and writer positioning by focussing on the linguistic resources of pronoun, mood and modality. We devised the following multiple choice questions to highlight the concept of language as choice and to make students aware of how the reader is positioned in the text:

How does the writer position herself/himself in the text?

> a) as 'I'
> b) as 'we'
> c) not obviously

Whose opinions are present in the text?

> a) the author's obviously
> b) the author's not obviously
> c) others

How does the text invite you to respond as a reader?

> a) as a receiver of facts
> b) as a receiver of opinion
> c) as someone who needs to answer a question
> d) as someone who needs to take action
> e) not at all

To what degree does the text obligate the reader to respond?

> a) strongly (must)
> b) encouraging (should)
> c) optional (could)

What degree of certainty does the writer attach to her/ his claims?

> *a) very sure (it is)*
> *b) somewhat tentative (it would be)*
> *c) uncertain (it may be)*

Using these questions and the assessor's comments gave us a good starting point for implementing critical reading practices. When, however, we attempted to apply the same questions to the student's own writing, their responses were minimal and did not result in critical writing practices. One student, for example, in response to the questions above indicated he had positioned his readers as a receiver of facts; but when he was asked how this might be changed he replied, 'it can't'. His response showed us that significantly more scaffolding was required to help him and others in the class see their own texts as involved in either asserting or contesting relations of power. This insight was later taken up and used by Tammi and Bronwyn who began their teaching after David and I. It also highlighted the limitations of worksheets in that they tend to create a checklist. They construct critical literacy as simply a new set of rules which, if followed correctly, will result in a perfectly composed, critically written essay.

As I reflect on my own struggles implementing critical literacy practices in the classroom, I believe they emerged not only from my inexperience and positioning as student teacher, but also from my need to believe what I was doing was useful. What was not useful for me was to see critical literacy as a 'magic formula' or 'magic bullet' (Lankshear 1994) which will fulfil all requirements and solve all problems in one swift stroke. The difficulty with this way of thinking is that it adopts critical literacy uncritically. Twelve months, many writing workshop sessions and two attempts to implement these ideas into classrooms later, my blind faith in critical literacy has been modified and replaced with a belief in its potential as a lens through which we question, reposition and deconstruct—a per-

spective from which critical literacy itself should not be excluded.

TAMMI AND BRONWYN: COLOURED UNDERLINES AND 'DO YOU BUY IT?'

Tammi and Bronwyn were located in a year 9 English classroom in an independent girls' school in the eastern suburbs of Melbourne where students were studying Shakespeare's *The Merchant of Venice*. Their supervising teacher was a respected leader in professional associations and encouraging of innovation. Before moving to the classroom Tammi and Bronwyn attempted to define more precisely what they meant by 'critical writing' by using three key principles identified by Comber (1994) to guide teacher action:

- repositioning students as researchers of language
- respecting student resistance and exploring minority culture constructions of literacy and language use
- problematising classroom and public texts

Tammi and Bronwyn were asked to develop a two-week unit that taught students to write a persuasive essay on *The Merchant of Venice*. They developed a number of metalinguistic strategies for making positioning visible in text, extending my work with Sasha in chapter 4 for use with a much larger group of students and 'solving' some of Karen's earlier dilemmas with worksheets. Tammi and Bronwyn write:

The students had identified two major issues in The Merchant *before we arrived, those of 'racism' and the 'role of women.' They had not, however, linguistically examined the text for the particular ways in which characters and ideas were constructed. We therefore decided to follow a traditional thematic approach to the text, but one that would ask different sorts of questions than those which are traditionally asked of the canon.*

We soon realised that in order to move students from reading other people's texts critically to reading their own writing critically, we needed to work directly with and on the students' own writing. Our first bit of concrete structural work was achieved not through contrived worksheets, but through a strategy we called 'coloured underlines', intended to lead directly to revision on the students' texts.

We 'invented' the technique through a discussion we had while marking the students' papers. We decided to underline examples of students' pronoun use, modality and discussion of text as a representation in specified colours to highlight particular patterns of usage. For us, this was an analytical tool to better understand how the student texts were constructed and how we might intervene. As soon as we realised how worthwhile the practice was for our own use, however, we knew we had to offer it to the students as well.

To introduce the strategy, we worked as a whole class and modelled sentences from some of the students' texts on the overhead projector and asked very simple questions. In regards to modality, we asked 'Do you buy it?' By this phrase we meant, Was the statement plausible or believable, was it able to be supported by evidence from the text? Alternately, was it too extreme an assertion, did it require qualifying or toning down? If students didn't 'buy it', they offered a more acceptable way of saying the same thing and we examined the effect of their suggested revision. This technique of drawing students' attention to particular linguistic strategies such as modality was intended to position them as more critical readers of their own texts.

We told students that the coloured underlines were not corrections and did not indicate that the modality should be changed. Rather, the underlines were to draw their attention to the ways they had used modality in their writing to express degrees of certainty or possibility. Students recognised that the objective was to utilise modality in a way which would be acceptable to readers (and eventually examiners); this was why we used the question 'Do you buy it?' to create a different reading reposition for students to assess their proffered argument. To illustrate, here is one student's revisions based on coloured underlines which dealt with modality.

FIRST DRAFT

They were given no power at all, therefore the men made all the decisions and held all the power in society.

REVISED DRAFT

Shakespeare gives the majority of the power to men, while women have very little power.

We also used the coloured underlines to highlight the constructed nature of text. Again using the overhead projector and examples of student writing we first asked questions such as 'Does the character seem like a real person here?' or Does this statement give Shakespeare responsibility for the character's actions?' By the end of the modelling session, nearly all students were making thoughtful revisions to their first drafts, as in the following example:

FIRST DRAFT

An example of this is when Portia and Nerissa had to dress up as males to get into the court and give their own opinion. This just shows how much power men had over women.

SECOND DRAFT

An example of this is the scene in which Portia and Nerissa had to dress up as males to get into the court and give their own opinion. This just shows how much power Shakespeare gave men over women.

The coloured underlines strategy seemed to give students the extra scaffolding needed to go from reading how power relations are constructed in another person's text to recognising these same aspects in their own texts. We were influenced here by the experience of Dave and Karen, whose students learned to identify such power relationships in other people's texts, but were less successful identifying them in their own.

Our early experimentation suggests that students were not only able to make thoughtful, critical revisions, but were also developing tools to analyse modality, pronouns, and language as representation within drafts of future texts. Once established, this strategy could be used to highlight other linguistic features of students' texts, such as nominalisation or mood.

We were successful to the extent that some students learned to highlight power relations rather than reproduce them unreflectively. They understood the importance of maintaining a coherent structure within the dominant conventions of persuasive writing, but they became aware that they were utilising conventions in order to gain authority within the dominant discourse. Students were thus 'repositioned as researchers of language', and began to understand their complicity in perpetuating the dominant discourse when choosing to reproduce power relations as given.

A POSTSCRIPT

A major limitation of most approaches to personal writing in school contexts is that questions of the personal remain untheorised. Teachers are frequently encouraged to cultivate the expression of the writer's authentic voice, but rarely is that voice located within larger social and cultural constructs (Dixon 1995) or seen to contribute to social injustices. Bronwyn, Tammi, David and Karen challenged such approaches by connecting issues of power with the teaching of writing; by making issues of power, positioning and representation as central as communication, clarity and truth.

A critical discourse analytic frame operated at many levels in their work. It provided a lens to help them read discourses in their own writing; to deconstruct revered cultural texts, such as those written by Shakespeare or the Victorian

Board of Studies; and to analyse both their success and failure as student teachers trying to implement a pedagogy that politicises the language classroom. Clearly they experienced the conflicts and contradictions of taking up this frame—the difficulties, for example, of trying to use linguistics critically. As their own writing demonstrates, however, they have also been repositioned as researchers, not simply as right or wrong or inexperienced, but as young professionals who have a great deal to teach a wider community of teachers and academics.

Student teachers are uniquely positioned to extend our knowledges about projects like critical literacies which come with no predetermined scripts and need to be defined and redefined in practice (Comber and Kamler 1997). If, as educators, we create more research spaces for students to work critically and collaboratively, they will be better positioned to teach as well as learn. The resistance student teachers may face when out in schools is something we also need to anticipate and work with differently. For unless we can open up new spaces where young teachers can challenge dominant discourses of literacy teaching, there is little hope of critical writing practices ever being explored or implemented.

Chapter Six

Language, Gender, Writing

This chapter foregrounds the cultural autobiographies written by two students in my Language, Gender and Education Master's course. Karina and Alice wrote their stories as part of an assignment that asked them to write disruptively—to insert 'the personal' into academic spaces where it is often silenced. Following Walkerdine (1990), we can regard these stories as fiction rather than truth, as attempts to rewrite the place of women in a patriarchal gender order.

> Is there an authentic female voice? For me the answer lies not, as some feminists have suggested, in some kind of essential feminine voice that has been silenced, but in that which exists in the interstices of our subjugation. We can tell other stories. These stories can be very frightening because they appear to blow apart the fictions through which we have come to understand ourselves. Underneath stories of quiet little girls are murderous fantasies. These are not there because they are essential to the female body or psyche but because the stories of our subjugation do not tell the whole truth: our socialization does not work. (Walkerdine 1990:xiv)

I begin with Alice and Karina's stories in order to allow the power of their narrative, undiluted by the commentary and framing I will provide subsequently. Each story is comprised of several scenes or parts. Together they comprise a larger story—a collective biography of the complexity and pain of mothering, a story which moves beyond the particular individuals who wrote the story, to the social and discursive processes which narrate the experience of being/becoming a mother.

The first story was written by Alice as a set of three discontinuous scenes. The original text was considerably longer and has been edited (other scenes have been omitted) with Alice's permission for the purposes of this chapter.

ALICE SPEAKS WITH HER THREE SISTERS-IN-LAW IN THE KITCHEN ON THE SUBJECT OF FEMALE CIRCUMCISION

> Alice: 27-year-old teacher, mother of newborn, isolated, clever, depressed
> Siti: 29-year-old architect, mother of three boys, chic, wealthy, sheltered, trapped
> Rohani: 36-year-old business woman, feisty, frustrated mother of two boys
> Katijah: 48-year-old crone, epileptic, plain, single, at times mad, embarrassing

A: Si, could I ask you something very personal?

Si: (cautiously) Yes.

A: Can I ask you about circumcision? Can you tell me what happens, what they do?

Si: (growing very cautious) Me? Why me? I know nothing about things like this. You should ask Emak.

A: Well, I can't. I was hoping you could tell me, especially since, you know, you've had it done, haven't you?

Si: Of course! (growing irritated) What a question! But I don't remember. I have boys. I've never seen it done. Why do you want to know?

A: Well you know that Emak brought it up about Erika.

Si: Yes, why? What's the problem? Don't you want to do it? Talk to your husband, lah! (suddenly

softening and laughing) Alice, Alice, sometimes
you are so funny . . .

A: He won't talk about things like this! But I was
reading that you don't have to in Islam that it's
not absolutely essential, isn't that right? (ner-
vousness now showing)

Si: (growing tense) It is! We don't have a choice
(she looks around for help from Rohani).

Ro: No Si, we do. Strictly speaking, we do (speaking with authority).

Si: (expressing disbelief) Since when?

Ro: It's advised, not required, but, you see, it's a
custom. We all do it. If you don't no one will
marry her (laughing). You have to (the two sis-
ters-in-law exchange guarded looks).

A: Well do you know what happens?

Ro: Listen, all I know is that it was done to me
long ago. I suppose you also want to ask me if
I enjoy sex as much as you, too. Well, how can
I tell?

Si: Men do it too! It gives you grace. Doesn't it?

Ro: Mmm. I'll tell you something. They don't do it
on the East Coast and you know the stories
about women from there! (giving a saucy look
and giggling)

A: Well, no I don't. What do you mean? I've heard
they're good business women.

Ro: (the women laugh) That's one way of putting
it. Well, they're supposed to be more powerful,
more (searching for a word) hot! You know what
I mean (laughing). Maybe that's the reason. But
I'll tell you (whispering) whatever they did to
me, I still like sex.

Katijah who has been taking her shoes off at the
door and listening, enters the kitchen.

Ka: So, Lady Di, you want to know about sunat!
snip! snip! snip! (Katijah dances around Alice
macabrely, laughing, with an imaginary pair of
scissors) Good. You don't want to stay dirty all
your life do you? Be clean like us.

Ro: Ish! disgusting! Kak' please!

Ka: What's wrong? Rahim's wife from America did it. Why not her? Anyway Emak wants you to do Erika soon (Alice becomes visibly nervous).

Si: (pats Alice's leg, whispering) Allah! Alice, ignore her.

Ka: Lady Di, listen to me. Do it now while she is too young to know. Don't be like me. 8 years old! They had to chase me all around Kampong Bahru and I screamed so loud that you could hear me in Kajang (Katijah laughs then becomes serious). Listen to Emak.

ALICE ATTEMPTS TO TALK ABOUT THE SUBJECT WITH A PAEDIATRICIAN

Dr De Marco: Come in my dear, please sit down. Now, you are . . .?

Alice: Alice Tyrone, Haji Razali's . . .

Dr De Marco: Ah yes, Razali's daughter-in-law. Yes! Did you know that we were school-mates at Victoria Institute? He played hockey for Malaysia. Did you know? Yes. A fine fellow. Now you are here to show me this charming little lady, and her name is . . . ?

Alice: Erika.

Dr De Marco: Erika, Erika what a pretty little girl you are. Yes. (He examines Erika's movement, breathing, responses, etc.) Well, you appear very healthy indeed little Erika. Feeding going well? No problems with milk? Good. Weight gain? Excellent. Now is there anything you want to discuss with me my dear?

Alice: Yes doctor, I would like to ask about the Malay custom of circumcision.

Dr De Marco: (grimacing and rising to his feet) Oh dear (walks to the window and starts to clean his glasses). You expatriate women do get hysterical about this

| | don't you? I've had you in here cry-
ing, shouting, goodness me! Where
did you say you were from my dear? |
| Alice: | Sydney, Doctor. |
| Dr De Marco: | Ah, I have two daughters in Perth
you know, excellent place Sydney,
many colleagues there doing damn
fine things in Paediatrics. Now my
dear, a word of advice from an old
man. Let the family do this! They
will love you for it. Pay no attention to this nonsense in the western
press of butchery and so on. I have
observed several of these procedures
as a young doctor in the villages.
These women know what they are
doing. Make no mistake about it.
This is not some maiming, disfigur-
ing procedure, no! It is a simple cut,
sometimes a scrape only, do you see.
There is minimal trauma, and little
bleeding. It varies of course. There
are some slight risks of tetanus and
so on, but I think you will find that
with these upper classes like your
husband's people, these people are
doing this for ritual. Please do not
worry yourself. OK now, my dear, is
there anything else? Good, excellent.
A pleasure to meet you my dear.
Give my kind regards to your father-
in-law. |

A LETTER FROM ALICE TO ERIKA

There were many other conversations my dearest
Erika, too many to describe in detail. The Dutch
nurse doing research for example, someone to whom
I should have been able to speak freely. Instead I
found myself inventing a needy friend who wanted
information. The judgmental female colleagues at
school who had no idea their words hit so close
when they said 'women who allow that to happen

should have their children removed by the welfare department'.

The Tasmanian woman, also married to a Malay, who was so subsumed by the society that she now spoke broken, Malay English. 'I have five daughters and I've had each one done. Its a blessing! They will be less burdened by sexual thoughts. Just make sure the woman isn't too old. She needs steady hands'.

There were Malay female friends who, though circumcised, could tell me nothing. Fauziah, for example, who had held her screaming daughter's knees apart but saw nothing because she was unable to bring herself to look or even to open her eyes. There was mid-forties, crazy Lucy, into every kind of fashionable therapy. 'Be outraged Alice!! Scream and shout! You must be your daughter's advocate!'

Then Erika there was Azizah, the only Malay woman I have known who categorically refused to have it done to her daughter Teja, named after the one female warrior in Malay mythology. Azizah and I became close allies, comparing notes, following up leads, both determined to know SOMETHING about this practice. Her confidence spurred me on. She was a professional advocate, a US trained lawyer and it showed. One day she called at school. 'Can you meet me 3 o'clock tomorrow at the Perkim Centre? I've found these Dakwah (fundamentalist) female doctors who work in a free women's clinic. It's ironic that they (the heavily veiled ones) should want to help, but they're willing to talk about it, show diagrams and so forth. What's more, they say it's NOT Islamic at all.'

We were jubilant! I felt immediate relief from the mounting anxiety that had plagued me since that first conversation with Emak. They wouldn't argue with Al Qur'an! I stopped off at the plaza to celebrate with Azizah—facials, followed by triple fudge sundaes at Swenson's Icecream parlour. It was trivial and mindless and it felt good.

As I walked into the kitchen I noticed the smell of burning incense. It was Thursday evening. The night Datuk burns incense to purify the house. In the dining room were the remains of a lavish tea party—tiny cakes, rendang, fried noodles, wild rice pudding and brown sugar syrup. Emak had put out her finest linen and the large lounge area had been cleared of furniture and covered in Persian carpets. They'd had a kenduri, a prayer meeting. 'I wonder who died?' I thought. Bowls of rose scented pot pouri lay on the kitchen table.

I saw Ayah, dressed in his Baju Melayu, coming slowly down the stairs.

'Alice, please come and sit down. I'd like to talk to you.' Always charming he was being extremely so today. 'Alice, today we had a special ceremony for Erika. We said some special prayers to soften her nature and then we had the Sunat ceremony. We didn't want to trouble you and Nordin because you are both so busy. Your great aunt and many of our relatives were here. It was very nice. She hardly cried.' He walked away.

I crumbled in a heap inside. I couldn't hide my devastation.

Where is she? Where's Nordin? I combed the house, my mind going at 100 miles an hour. There were no words for the rage I felt. Had he known? Did he just let it happen without telling me? Eventually I found Katijah walking with you in the orchid garden. 'Give her to me!' I screamed. I walked back and forward sobbing with utter frustration. Furious with myself for failing you. Furious with your father for not supporting me. Furious with the family for their quiet, elegant Malay arrogance. Furious with this dishonest, duplicitous society. You were just eight months old.

Like Fauziah I found I could not look. I took off your nappy with shaking hands but I dared not look, yet. What good would it do? They had made their mark, as surely as graffiti engraved on wood or stone. But also they had claimed you through the ritual. Witnessed by all but me. You have been tempered.

For many months I shuddered at my own impotence. I became deeply disturbed and very anxious. I started to have strange psychological experiences, I would look in the mirror, recognise myself, but be unable to summon any sense of self awareness. Though I went through the daily rituals and appeared to be functioning, I knew that I was becoming invisible. It would be another three years before I found the strength to break away.

We are watching Foreign Correspondent. A black African girl is being led, eyes glazed with fear, towards her gruesome circumcision. It is extreme, grotesque and in no way subtle like yours. You are mesmerised by this story. 'Disgusting! Gross! Why?' you say. 'How could anyone allow that to happen to their daughter?'

The next story was written by Karina and consists of four parts: two birthing stories and two sets of commentaries. Like Alice, Karina explores mothering, but from the position of one giving birth to a daughter and a son. Like Alice, she juxtaposes and works across a number of different genres. I have represented her first-person account in italics, and her third-person reading of the same story in Roman font. This juxtaposition calls attention to the way in which the story is written, reminding the reader that this is indeed a fiction, a representation, where the writer Karina is made visible and referred to alternately as *I, the woman, her*. It demonstrates that even in autobiographical narrative, the narrator is a position, an angle of vision and not simply the student confessing his or her authentic feelings or truths.

BIRTHING STORY: THE FIRST

From the waist down, my body was numb. I watched as the contractions etched a pattern of undulating waves on the monitor beside the bed. The doctor entered, dressed as a vet, in rubber gloves, apron and boots.

'Let's get this baby out,' she said.

The team launched into action. Equipment was wheeled in, people appeared busily donning masks, gloves and protective clothing. My legs were elevated and my ankles bound to stirrups.

'We'll have to do an episiotomy,' said the doctor.

My perineum was duly cut. Visions of a natural, drug free birth had long ago dissolved. How many days had I been in labour? My sense of time was obliterated. All I could do now was not die. I wanted to see my baby.

'PUSH,' urged the midwife.

'You're going to have to push as hard as you can,' the doctor instructed. In her hand she held a pair of metal tongs, forceps They looked cold, menacing, an instrument of torture. The midwife pressed down on my abdomen with her entire weight. The doctor's face was turning purple. The veins in her neck bulged. I was the victim of an obscene dental nightmare. My centre was being ripped out of my body.

'You're going to have to push harder,' said my husband.

Without any localised sensations it was impossible to know what to push, so pushing everything I had, my baby was dragged out of me. The midwife placed the child on my chest, her face towards me. We locked eyes. I travelled into blue eternity. I knew her, as intimate and stranger.

In this story the woman is constituted as object. Her body is 'numb' from the waist down, she is detached from her body as she watches the contractions on a screen. Within the discourse of obstetrics, there exists no legitimate place for the expression of emotion so she does not allow herself to explore the implications of this situation, so different from the birth she has imagined. The machine is master, telling her of her body's labours.

The woman is positioned and named victim. The reader is positioned to understand the practices of the doctor as a violation of the woman's body. Her legs are 'elevated 'and 'bound'. The baby is 'dragged' and 'ripped' from the woman's body. In this position she is powerless, it is the doctor and the medical team who are in control of this birth. The epidural anaesthetises her lower body and allows the doctor to assume control. The woman can only act in the negative. 'All I could do now was not die . . . '

A contradictory reading of the story might be produced if the woman's survival of this ordeal was foregrounded—an heroic tale of endurance in the face of sinister manifestations of medical/gynaecological discourse. In order for such a reading to be produced, the writer would have to include issues on which she chose to be silent; the difficulty of the birth, her sense of failure at having to seek refuge in drugs, the terror of the powerlessness, her shock at the damage the birth process inflicted on her daughter. Such a reading goes against the grain. But in viewing the story through the lens of feminist poststructuralism, the writer realises she has been carrying the weight of silence around this birth as personal failure.

The pain is an integral element of the birthing process. Not experienced at the time, it resurfaces in the week following the birth as mind-searing headache and in the recreation of the experience in text, it resurfaces as the most excruciating toothache I have ever experienced. My dentist calls it neuralgia. My jaw is clenched and tense. The body remembers when the mind does not. On writing about the birth I am forced to confront the pain, the pain of giving birth to my story. The constriction I experience in my jaw is the constriction of my uterus, as I struggled to give birth against the grain in a place where female sexuality was denied.

The fear of being rendered powerless in the labour ward is translated into a fear of narrating my story. I give birth to text as frightening and painful and exhilarating as giving birth to a child. In telling my first birth story can I reposition myself as powerful? It is I who birthed this child.

BIRTHING STORY: THE SECOND

The woman had been cleaning manically for days. The house was a shrine: flowers perfectly positioned, nappies folded, drawers neatly stacked with tiny clothes. She was ready. She was in bed when the contractions started. Rhythmically they punctuated her dozing. As it grew light they came closer together, but manageable. She had all the time in the world before they needed to move to the birthing centre. Nevertheless, her husband arranged to meet the midwife at the birthing centre later in the afternoon.

She floated, relaxed in the bath, marvelling at her hugeness, relieved that the birth was imminent. When she returned to her bedroom, the contractions were sharper, closer together. She began to pace the room, stopping with each contraction to pant and rock her hips in time with her breath, an intense, concentrated belly dance. She was drawing in on herself, summoning her energies.

She wanted her midwife NOW, *needed the reassurance of a female presence. Her husband paged the midwife. The woman found herself on all fours, kneeling over the bed. Her head was buried in the bed, pillows muffling her screams. The force of the pain obliterated her. The wild energy was her power to birth. She wanted her midwife.*

'I can see the head!' the husband said.

She was encouraged. She wanted her midwife. The woman giving birth embodied creation and destruction. She heard a knock at the front door. Her midwife. Now she could allow her baby passage into the world. With the next contraction, her baby was born.

The child lay motionless on the floor. Eyes closed, head blue, cord spiralled with red veins, body a deep magenta. The woman watched, from a great distance.

'Your baby's alright.' The midwife answered the unspoken question. 'He just needs a bit of help.'

She watched as the midwife breathed into the tiny mouth. He began to cry. Loud, angry, insistent. She held him. His cries filled the room. His eyes remained shut. Who was he?

This story disrupts the medical discourse of birthing by situating the birth within the home. The woman does not consciously decide on a home birth; medical discourses of birthing define the hospital as the site where birth can be controlled, monitored and rendered 'safe'. Nevertheless, the woman has been preparing the birth place by meticulous cleaning. Her home has become a sacred space, a 'shrine' within which to welcome the child; all is 'perfectly positioned' and 'ready'. The birth imperative, however, side steps the necessity of making a rational decision to leave home for the birth centre. The child will be born in the place where he was conceived.

The woman is relaxed and at ease; she has discovered the traditional support of birthing women: water, rhythmical movement and sacred personal space; an age-old wisdom has emerged in her body. The midwife is the wise woman who operates outside the patriarchal medical discourse. The woman demands her presence for 'reassurance'; it is not until the midwife arrives that the woman gives birth. It is the midwife who initiates the infant's first breath with her own. Her presence is crucial.

The woman in this story is positioned as powerful. Her power comes from within; the pain 'obliterated her' and still she is the embodiment of contradiction; creation and destruction exist within her simultaneously. She is the power to give birth and she gives birth to what appears, momentarily, to be death. The male child is positioned in the story as Other. The mother observes him 'from a great distance'. His cries are 'loud, angry insistent'. The reader is positioned to see the crying infant as stranger. He does not connect with the mother but remains closed to her. By contrast, the meeting of the mother with the female child is represented as connection. As the two connect their gaze they fuse in a mystical knowledge of the other, even though the child is simultaneously 'stranger' . . . .

During the writing of the final draft I have a dream of a friend and colleague. I have always been impressed and a little in awe of her forthright commitment to feminism. In the dream she has joined me in a new workplace. She presents her opinion on a matter of policy with clarity and passion. I interpret this dream as an image of myself as speaking subject. Through the challenge of writing this piece I have confronted my silences. I have found myself speaking stories for the first time.

A FEMINIST POSTSTRUCTURALIST
DISTANCE PEDAGOGY

The pedagogy that scaffolded these stories was located within a feminist poststructuralist paradigm. Students such as Karina and Alice, who enrolled in my Language, Gender and Education course read a number of theorists who regard language as constitutive of self and experience itself as gendered by a complex set of social and cultural practices.

One of the most distinctive aspects of this pedagogy was its structuring as distance off-campus learning. The students were mostly women, mostly practising teachers in elementary, secondary, university, adult, ESL and workplace contexts engaged in part-time Master's degrees as mid-career development. They were scattered around the vast distance that is Australia and in such overseas locations as Singapore, Japan, Pakistan and Thailand. The university where they enrolled had a long tradition of distance education, although in recent years notions of flexible learning, new technologies and lifelong learning have reshaped most Australian universities in the 1990s so that they incorporate forms of distance learning using online technologies.

What this meant in 1993, however, when the course was first designed, was that I spent a great deal of time constructing high-quality print and audiovisual materials, including: a study guide (lecture and discussion notes on issues and readings in the course), a unit guide (assignment details and administrative procedures), two commissioned monographs by feminist poststructuralist educators (*Gender Stories and the Language Classroom* by Pam Gilbert and *Poststructuralist Theory and Classroom Practice* by Bronwyn Davies); a course reader (exemplars of disruptive feminist fiction), two audiotaped conversations (between myself, Pam Gilbert and Bronwyn Davies on feminist poststructural theorising in education and with Alison Lee on critical discourse analysis), and a set text (*Feminist Practice and Poststructuralist Theory* by Chris Weedon).

As students wrote in isolation from the group, my distance pedagogy constructed as much contact as possible, given financial and physical constraints. I invited students to engage in three teleconferences during the semester, where groups of six to eight students met with me over the phone to discuss issues of feminist poststructuralist theory, practice and writing. These were supplemented by phone calls from students, usually to discuss their two major assignments.

The second teleconference was particularly challenging as it was structured as a writing conference. Students were divided into groups of six and required to forward a draft of their cultural autobiography to all group members prior to the teleconference. They could use email, mail or fax depending on the technologies available to them. As coordinator of the conference, I orchestrated a complex set of logistic moves to ensure that all students were prepared to respond to drafts during the teleconference. While the phone is certainly not an ideal context for a writing conference, I believed it was better than not having students engage in collective critique.

The conference itself was shaped by a poststructuralist theoretical position which challenged commonplace views of how readers construct meaning. I asked students to view the draft as contradictory and fragmentary and the conference itself as an opportunity to produce a variety of readings. A number of suggested questions were used to guide the conference, based on the work of Bronwyn Mellor, Annette Patterson and Marnie O'Neill in *Reading Fictions* (1991) and Wayne Martino and Bronwyn Mellor in *Gendered Fictions* (1995). Some of these included:

- What parts of the text or textual fragments are emphasised or foregrounded?
- What textual fragments are privileged or read as most important?
- What textual fragments are ignored, marginalised or silenced?
- How are particular textual fragments read to 'fit' a reading?
- What are the possible readings that can be produced from this text?

As most student texts had been circulated and read prior to the conference, we assigned ten minutes to each student's text for long-distance response and deconstruction. These are, of course, awkward discursive events, given that no one has ever sighted the body of the writer and time limitations make it impossible to explore the depth and immediacy possible in face-to-face encounters. Nevertheless, most students found the response useful in calming their anxiety, in reading their text against others in the group and seeing the power of binary thinking in constructing gendered subjectivities. Some even found pleasure in the anonymity of the encounter—the bodiless voice, the disembodied text of distance education.

WRITING NEW STORYLINES

While the course materials privileged poststructural feminist thinking and opted for an in-depth treatment of one perspective rather than a survey course, the study guide encouraged students to explore the multiplicity of feminisms and the variety of categories used by feminist theorists to position and describe these, including: liberal, Marxist, socialist radical (Jaggar 1983); liberal, Marxist, radical, psychoanalytic (Tong 1989); liberal, radical, socialist, poststructuralist (Kenway 1991).

> For feminist educators, feminism is a primary lens through which the world is interpreted and acted upon. Of course, feminism is not a monolithic discourse. There are, in fact, many feminisms informed by various social theories and research traditions and motivated by somewhat different social, political and educational projects, each experiencing their own theoretical and practical problems. . . . While feminism is certainly driven by a vision of a world which might be otherwise, the vision depends on the type of feminism which is being espoused. (Kenway and Modra 1992:139)

In order to investigate what poststructuralist theorising might mean for feminism, for education, for writing pedagogy, I encouraged students to investigate discourses of post-structuralism through Chris Weedon's text, *Feminist Practice and Poststructuralist Theory* (1987) and my study guide notes.

> Poststructuralism is a term applied to a very loosely connected set of ideas about meaning, the way in which meaning is struggled over and made, the way it circulates amongst us, the impact it has on human subjects and finally, the connections between meaning and power. For poststructuralists, meaning is not fixed in language or in other cultural symbols and neither is it fixed in consistent power relationships. It shifts according to the ways in which a range of linguistic, institutional and cultural factors come together. It is influenced and influences shifting patterns of power. And finally, it constitutes human subjectivity which is, again, regarded as shifting, many-faceted and contradictory. . . . Such a view of meaning then, calls attention to the particular rather than the general, to discontinuity and instability rather than continuity and stability, to plurality, diversity and difference rather than to similarity and commonality and to the complex and multi-faceted rather than the essential. (Kenway 1992:5, in study guide)

Different feminisms have different ways of theorising language with different consequences for writing and social action. Implicit in the two assignments I set students was the belief that a feminist poststructuralist view of language was the most productive for transformative (social/individual) work. In the first assignment students were asked to write a cultural autobiography; in the second, they were asked to analyse the construction of gendered subjectivities in classroom discourse. In this chapter I examine only the first assignment, of which Karina and Alice's texts are two examples.

The assignment was divided into two parts. In the first part, students selected some aspect(s) of their life experience as a springboard for theorising the construction of gendered subjectivity. They examined the gendered nature of writing practices and attempted to create new storylines, new metaphors (much as the older women did in chapter 3) which position women and men differently. In the second part, they examined the writing they produced, its process of production, and the possible reading positions it offered. Further, they discussed the difficulties encountered in trying to disrupt dominant discourses and write outside dualistic oppositions of femininity and masculinity.

To frame the assignment in such terms was to take issue with some of the linguistic and political assumptions of radical feminism, in particular notions of linguistic determinism and male control of language, articulated in extreme form by such theories as Spender's (1980) man-made language. Radical feminists like Dale Spender, who emphasise the alienation of women's experience in patriarchy, often target language as a major source of that alienation. Spender has argued that women who speak and write in a man-made symbolic universe are women alienated from language. Women without the ability to symbolise their experience in the male language are seen to have few choices; they can either internalise male reality or find themselves silenced— unable to say anything.

Like Deborah Cameron (1992), I regard such linguistic theorising as inadequate and pessimistic, emphasising as it does women's exclusion, alienation and marginality, on the one hand, while celebrating their difference, on the other, with the same patriarchal language that oppresses them. Such a conception leaves little space for agency, for seeing women as active social and linguistic agents, except paradoxically—in reversing the symbolic order, and thereby keeping it intact. I attempted, instead, to use my assignment as a vehicle for relocating students in Kristeva's third tier of feminism.

In her article *Women's Time* (1986), Kristeva articulates a three-tier stage of feminisms: a first stage, where women demand equality with men and seek to gain insertion into the symbolic order (*liberal feminism*); a second stage, in which the male symbolic order is rejected, and women seek to 'give a language to the intrasubjective and corporeal experiences left mute by culture in the past' (1986:194) (*radical femi-*

nism); and a third stage, which rejects the dichotomy between male and female and seeks to transcend the dualistic gendered order. While Kristeva's 'clear preference is for the attitude toward women made possible within the third tier . . . she argues that each tier or stage should have a "parallel existence" in the same historical time, or even be "interwoven one with the other" (Kristeva 1986:209, in Gilbert 1993a:7).

Cameron (1992:39) argues that most contemporary feminist politics oscillate somewhere between the first and second stages, deploring and celebrating difference, without expecting to transcend gender differences. While the third stage is clearly utopian, it is the space where I ask students to write, if for no other reason than to help them understand how deeply the male/female binary is written into body, text and culture; how it is created and sustained through writing; and how difficult it is to disrupt rather than simply reverse a whole set of binary oppositions (male/female, strong/weak, rational/irrational, mind/body, light/dark, public/private) that organise Western logic.

Such a task does not disavow work that occurs in Kristeva's first two tiers—stories that name inequality or that search for female valuation and celebrate difference. It does, however, recognise the importance of working *with* rather than rejecting the language/stories through which gendered subjectivity is constituted. The exploratory and experimental nature of this writing positions students in a manner similar to Tammi, Bronwyn, Karen and David in chapter 5—not as right or wrong, but as researchers in a larger sociopolitical linguistic project, which includes but extends beyond them.

> Whether women can, by breaking silence, by speaking and writing, help overcome binary oppositions, phallocentrism, and logocentrism, I do not know. All that I know is that we humans could do with a new conceptual start. In our desire to achieve unity, we have excluded, ostracised, and alienated so-called abnormal, deviant, and marginal people. As a result of this policy of exclusion, we have impoverished the human community. We have, it seems, very little to lose and much to gain by joining a variety

of postmodern feminists in their celebration of multiplicity. For even if we cannot all be One, we can be Many. There may yet be a way to achieve unity in diversity. (Tong 1989:233)

MODELLING DISRUPTIVE FICTIONS

To write new stories in the third tier requires scaffolding and immersion in a whole set of stories that model new possibilities, new genres. Given the exploratory nature of the student writing task, it seemed important to provide a multiplicity of models of disruptive fictions, rather than valorise a particular way of writing. In a distance pedagogy, where there is no embodied space for collaborative work between teacher and student, no space for clay work of the kind I employed with Sasha in chapter 4, such models take on particular importance in supporting student writing.

There is a substantial body of feminist scholarship to call on in this regard, which goes by a variety of names including *narrative criticism* (Miller 1991) *autoethnography* (Brodkey 1996a and b), *cross genre writing* (Freedman 1992), *cultural biography* (Davies 1994) and *memory work* (Haug 1987). Feminist writers in a variety of locations (composition, women's studies, education, English) have theorised autobiographical writing in ways which move it beyond the personal, which encourage 'the intertwining of the private and public; the autobiographical and the theoretical; the meditative, and the pedagogical aspects of women's lives' (Schmidt 1998:2).

Sue Middleton (1993), for example, working in the sociology of women's education, uses autobiography as a way of engaging in cultural critique, of complicating students' sense of identity while engaging them in serious cultural analysis. Middleton argues the necessity of teachers making visible aspects of their own life histories by exploring intersections between individual biographies, historical events and the broader power relations that have contained and shaped our perspectives as educators.

Nancy Miller (1991) working in women's studies and literature, practices a brand of autobiographical writing she calls narrative criticism. In her view, the case *for* personal writing entails the reclaiming (rather than the rejection) of theory: 'turning theory back on itself' (Miller 1991:5). To produce new writing, to speak autobiographically in an academic context is to speak 'against a language of abstraction; against male theories that constitute women in lack, invisibility, silence' (Miller 1991:7).

Other feminist critics have relied on a self-conscious mixture of genres, using narrative, testimony, anecdote, poetry and essay—what Diane Freedman (1992) calls cross-genre writing—to revise the conventional academic modes they would criticise. 'By pushing against perceived . . . generic and literary boundaries, cross-genre writers try to translate and traverse borders usually considered more 'real' and material than literary' (Freedman 1992:15).

As a teacher of distance pedagogy, I called on this growing body of scholarship to construct a course reader of disruptive genres. The reader had at least two purposes: to work against universal assumptions about women as a unitary and undifferentiated group and to provide models of disruptive writing—that is, possible ways of breaking genre, challenging personal/political/theoretical boundaries and generating new positions from which to speak.

The idea of a unitary and universal category 'woman' has been challenged by women of colour for its racist assumptions, by working-class women for it classist assumptions, by lesbian women for its heterosexist assumptions and by poststructuralist feminist theorists who emphasise the contradictory, multiple and in-process nature of socially given identities such as *woman*. To encourage students to engage the politics of difference and the complexity of given social identities, the reader included texts by such feminist writers as Cherie Moraga and Gloria Anzaldua (1983), Audre Lorde (1984), Jackie Huggins (1992) and Valerie Walkerdine (1990).

It also included disruptive texts by academic writers in different sites, such as Patricia Williams (1991) in law, Nancy Miller (1991) in English, Valerie Walkerdine (1990) in psychology, and Carolyn Steedman (1986) in history to highlight the discipline–specific ways autobiography functions as cultural criticism. By introducing narratives of lived experience into their essays for the academy, these writers challenge readers to examine the 'central role social and historical practices play in shaping and producing these narratives' (Fuss 1989:118).

REFLECTING ON THE STORIES:
NOT HOWLING BUT SHAPING

To be authorised by the academy to write about one's life is a powerful and often startling experience for university students like Karina and Alice, disrupting as it does the personal/ impersonal, academic/nonacademic, objective/ subjective set of binaries that organise university life. In the second part of their assignments (not reproduced here), Karina and Alice provided critical reflections on the experience of writing and interacting with others about their texts, as required. Like other students who I have taught over the years, they emphasised the material effects of being allowed to write the personal into the academy.

To explore in greater depth the impact of the writing and their experience of the pedagogy, I also invited Karina and Alice to talk with me in an interview setting. As they both lived in Melbourne, it was possible to bring them together physically in the same space. This discussion was held in January 1996, two years after the writing, in preparation for writing this book. Karina and Alice did not know one another prior to the meeting as they had been enrolled in the Language, Gender and Education course in different semesters. Their conversation, mediated and shaped by my questions, was less a dialogue than a series of segmented monologues, with encouraging response and interjections and some building on one another's turns.

As I read and reread the transcript of my interview with Karina and Alice, I was struck by a number of similar themes (despite the very different texts they produced) organised around a set of binary oppositions: fiction/truth, constraint/ release, silence/voice, pain/relief. I divided the transcript into sections around these themes, pulling out appropriate phrases from different sections of the transcript, and soon found myself shaping a narrative from their words. In particular, I was taken with metaphors of outpouring and breaking silence because of my interest in the transformative power of this writing.

The question of how to present this narrative, how to represent Alice and Karina in and through the interview material troubled me. I wished to avoid overexplaining what Karina and Alice said and was dissatisfied with the idea of simply 'sandwiching the research subject's voice between my commentary' (Thomson 1997–98b:10). I also wanted to call attention to the fact that transcript data is already a representation of experience, rather than truth, and that it is *produced* by the researcher, rather than simply *found* (Reid *et al.* 1996).

I am influenced here by poststructural and narrative methods of research, in particular recent work by Thomson (1999) and Richardson (1997) which explores the potential of narrative to develop alternate ways of knowing and telling. Pat Thomson thinks of research as a literary process and experiments with a number of literary devices and techniques for data selection, analysis and re-presentation. In her doctoral dissertation Thomson (1999) disrupts the conventional sociological genre of third-person narrative, analytic prose and indented direct transcript quotations with what she calls 'acts of delinquent storying'—a borrowing of techniques of representation from other genres and disciplines.

The idea of transforming the dialogic transcript of Karina and Alice's interview into another genre was attractive to me, given my intention in this chapter and the Language and Gender course more broadly to work disruptively with genres of experience. Further, since the interview itself was designed to reflect on the process of producing disruptive texts, a disruptive genre seemed a highly appropriate way to write about such a conversation.

The technique developed by Laurel Richardson (1997) of creating poems from transcripts was of particular interest for its innovation in playing with pauses, line breaks, and spaces between lines and stanzas to create text that mimics the rhythms of conversation.

> By violating the conventions of how interviews are
> written up, those conventions are uncovered as

choices authors make, not rules for writing truths. The poetic form, moreover, because it plays with connotative structures and literary devices to convey meaning, commends itself to multiple and open readings in ways that straight sociological prose does not. . . . Knowledge is thus metaphored and experienced as prismatic, partial and positional, rather than single, total, unequivocal. (Richardson 1997:210)

Thomson (1997-98b) in her work with disadvantaged schools, elaborates further on the power/challenge of producing a transcript poem.

This is a confronting move, it pares down, hones what has been captured on tape to a narrative that tells both emotionally and intellectually. It creates a stand alone text from transcript rather than encasing the transcript extracts in commentary. It presents a story rather than having the story told. It does not present truth, but aims to re-present truthfulness. This approach has been labelled invalid, subjective trivial, and un-academic because it challenges the conventional norms of sociological selection and presentation. Yet all data collection is a process managed and manipulated by the researcher and all research texts are constructed through writing and reading. This method draws attention to the acts of the researcher in manipulating and selecting and makes them visible, un-natural, needing to be defended and explained. (Thomson 1997–98b:10)

To construct the transcript poem from the interview with Alice and Karina, I asked a number of questions about the transcript, including:

What is the dominant story being told?
What are the recurring themes?
Where is the repetition of phrase and rhythm?
Where are the silences, pauses, hesitations?

The poem I have constructed consists of four movements, each comprised of sentences I have selected around four narrative themes of outpouring, crafting, guilt, and release. Using Karina and Alice's exact words, but not necessarily in the chronological order they were spoken, I cut and pasted sentences from the twenty-five pages of transcribed conversation. Although I did not change their words, I sometimes pared them down, omitting phrases, articles (the, a), smoothing the text but trying to capture their spoken intonation and syntactic rhythm. In presenting their words, I distinguish between Karina and Alice's turns and locate them vertically down the page. One effect of this poetic representation is to create a greater sense of dialogue than occurred in the interview. I have omitted my initiating questions and response as interviewer from the text, but these operate, I believe, as an absent presence, as the unstated questions that shape the stories the women articulate.

In editing and paring down the transcript poem I experimented a great deal with line presentation, how to divide the lines for emphasis and recapture the embodied rhythm of the conversation. Richardson suggests that

> poetry can re-create embodied speech in a way that standard sociological prose does not because poetry consciously employs such devices as line length, meter, cadence, speed, alliteration, assonance, connotation, rhyme, off rhyme variation and repetition to elicit bodily responses in reader/listeners . . . lived experience is lived in a body and poetic representation can touch us where we live, in our bodies. (Richardson 1997:143)

TRANSCRIPT POEM: ALICE AND KARINA

outpouring, crying, spewing

A: It's an excruciating experience
utterly controlled by silence in me
but there is really no way that you can tell
this story

without fear of condemnation from many sides.
It was such a big thing to get past that churning
out of memory,
that personal outpouring thing was very hard.
But for me
the difference between just outpouring
is that you are just sort of   spewing it out
the outpouring is talking to yourself,
bringing it out
spewing it out
whereas in this case I was actually trying to
juxtapose things
arrange things to have impact.
So that's the difference for me,
mind you
I sat at the computer way into the night
crying a lot of the time,
and you know writing and wiping,
writing   and   wiping,   writing
and   wiping
to actually get past this outpouring thing.

K: The outpouring becomes the first stage
and it's a necessary stage
it's necessary to kind of explore the realms
you're getting into,
but it's raw
and it's agonising
and it's painful
but somehow something happens in the shift
to thinking about the reader
and thinking about an audience
that became some kind of
constraint
but the initial writing was very 'out there.'
I had never talked about it with anybody you know
I hadn't
talked about it in any kind of detail.

shaping, fictionalising, containing

K: Control
was
what

I
needed
to be able to tell the story.
I couldn't have actually told it
unless it was as clinical as it was,
as if I was out of my body and watching it happen.

A: I was creating a fiction
and there were these scenes that would help
contain it,
I don't know how to explain this
but I knew that I could build towards that end
and it would   get the reader
and there was a
sense
of
retaliation.
It was a reworking of the past
but in a fictional sense,
containing it in a number of words and scenes
and I felt I had to make it Erika's story
it was like this is
our   story
even though I haven't told her this story
yet.

The power of this writing is it allows you to accept
that you are reconstructing it.
And there is that   sense of
containment
that makes it possible to look at things that are
painful.
It's the naming of the experience or the condensing
that's part of the pleasure of it
playing with those elements
and recreating them with different words
but the same essence   you know what I mean
going for an essence in a way that is
truthful
but crafting it,
which is an empowering way to deal with your
experience
more so than just   blurting   it   out.

K: It does give it some sort of shape
it's like firing a piece of pottery in a furnace
and then you can paint it
and you can embellish it
but it's not going to crumble.

pain, failure, responsibility, guilt

K: Writing meant acknowledging the pain of it
and the disjuncture between my ideal and
the reality
the cultural ideal of glowing, beautiful mothers.
It meant that through the writing of it
I did not have to take it all on
as
my
own
failure
that the discourses from the natural, drug free births
were very strong amongst my peers and there was
a sense that if you didn't do that,
you were in some way inadequate.

Maybe I could only write about this because the
second birth was different,
the antithesis of the first.
In facing the fear that happened right through the
birth
and in the experience of writing it
I actually managed to articulate the horror
and in doing that
I found the strength or courage to then
move
beyond
me,
beyond the sense that I was pivotal
and see there were a whole lot of other influences,
that
it
just
wasn't
me
shaping the experience of birth
but it was also determined by cultural factors.

A: This would blow away people in Malaysia
that I have the audacity to write such a text
but I really learned a lot from doing this
more than I would if I had told it
in therapy
where someone else was directing the story
directing me
in the way I explored it.
I got a lot of pleasure,
well, a comfort from exploring it
I think I realised in the telling of it
it
wasn't
my
fault.

Of course
I am scared to say, 'Erika I let this happen to you',
well I didn't
it happened
it was done to her
not with my permission.
But I had that terrible sense of responsibility
so I am afraid to tell her about it,
but once it becomes text and it's published
I think I could
but I feel she needs to be perhaps just a bit older
perhaps that is just an excuse for me.

. . . and after the writing

K: I know for me this was sort of a conduit to
feelings that were living in me that hadn't been
explored and I relived them as I wrote.
I started bleeding
My tooth totally cracked in half while I was writing.
It was extraordinary.

A: It was soothing in a funny way for me
I read it and read it and read it and read it
and felt it was terribly important.

K: I share that sense of it being critical,
critical that it was done.
I think it shaped me in a powerful way
I'm not sure I can articulate how.
It needed to be told
and in some way the telling of it has
and will allow
further tellings
like this is the first stage of something.

A: It empowers you,
you resurrected a story, sort of ripped it out
and worked it,
worked it in a way and produced it.
I was very taken with the notion that this
experience has wider meaning for many women.
I got a lot of strength from that idea.
We are actually rewriting what is valued knowledge
what is a tradition worthy of being studied.
I mean we're moving in and giving shape to areas of
experience
which have not been given form in the academy
before.
But perhaps the journey is a fraught one.
It requires some trust and some courage
some ability to say
look
I
don't
care,
the gain I'm going to get from this is going to be
worth this agony
which is like no other.

K: In one sense through this writing
everything
is
different.
The world is coded very differently for me now.
I ask where am I positioned, who is speaking and
why are they speaking? What is their influence and
what is the genealogy of that perspective?

I can't accept anything as I used to before.
It has actually problematised everything in my life.
And I see now
that the way I saw gender being constructed was
totally simplistic
and in some ways   a complete fallacy,
you know   the taking for granted
that in being a mother of a girl
there was some sort of mystic union that wasn't
there with my son
it seems embarrassingly naive now
because I can see the construction of gender as
so
much
more
complex.

TRANSFORMING EXPERIENCE

The pedagogy developed in this chapter shares many of the
goals of a feminist pedagogy as these are articulated by
Kathleen Weiler (1994), including a commitment to a vision
of social change, to experience and feeling as a guide to theoretical understanding, and to the 'goal of making students
theorists of their own lives by interrogating and analyzing
their own experience' (Weiler 1994:26). Its emphasis on the
critical, however, is central. I have called it a critical writing
pedagogy rather than a feminist writing pedagogy because it
rests on a critical understanding of the forces that have shaped
women's experience—rather than using experience itself as a
guide to a deeper truth about women.

For Karina and Alice the experience of writing a cultural
autobiography transformed experience. Karina's text rewrote
her relation both to mothering and the pedagogy she later used
with her own women students. For Alice, who had not yet
told her daughter, a space was created to rehearse a telling she
could live with and imagine speaking. We can think of these
transformative moments as textually based relocations, brought
into being by the act of writing self-conscious critique and
reflection. The stories that result are not simply an outpour-

ing of emotion, a writing as therapy. They also function as a cultural critique of discourses of 'good mothering', realised differently in middle-class Australia and upper-class Malaysia.

In her discussion of the place of feeling and experience in feminist pedagogy, Weiler (1994) highlights the danger of confessional release for its own sake.

> One danger within a feminist pedagogy committed to the use of feeling or emotion and experience as a source of knowledge is that expression of strong emotion can simply be catharctic and may deflect the need for action to address underlying causes of that emotion. (Weiler 1994:27)

It seemed to me as I constructed the transcript poem, that strong emotion was an essential first part of the writing for Karina and Alice but not an end in itself. The initial release is catharctic and undisciplined. It is the unspoken, never-worded experience that struggles to be released, articulated into words, and it is accompanied by tears and wild, raw emotion.

The deliberate crafting and staging which follows, however, is a critical action, which contains and transforms emotion. That crafting functions as a shaping of text, emotion, subjectivity—a making of fiction that seeks to recapture the experience but forces the reader to engage with it in particular ways (eg, through multiple scenes, mixed genres, multiple voices). The act of writing and rewriting relocates the anguished howl in a new set of discourses, with material effects that are surprising to both women. As a consequence, their experience is remade and reread discursively as more than the failure of the individual. Without exonerating their own responsibility, they learn they need not carry all the blame themselves.

I regard this writing as a success, a tangible instance of Kress' notion of writing as a design for both text and subjectivity. Intensive and self-conscious critical work by Karina and Alice on the language through which they tell experience produced both a crafted text and positive effects on the writer's life. But their 'success stories' also raise a number of questions about the ways in which we treat experience in other sites of feminist pedagogy, such as women's studies or North American composition, where until recently there has been little attention to building models of feminist composition instruction (Flynn 1991). I am thinking, in particular, about the dangers of valorising experience rather than treating it critically or of simply equating a focus on experience with an emancipatory curriculum.

Such tendencies are evident in a collection edited by feminist compositionists Caywood and Overing (1987), where student-centred, process and expressive pedagogies are simply assumed to be feminist and emancipatory. While progressive pedagogies enacted in student-centred composition classrooms may partially enact feminist goals of displacing the authority of the teacher and shifting power to students, they also present problems for women and for feminism (see Jarratt 1991 for a similar argument).

The editors claim, for example, that 'the process model, insofar as it facilitates the fullest expression of the individual voice, is compatible with the feminist revision of hierarchy, if not essential to it' (Caywood and Overing 1987:xiv). One writer in the collection asks: How does a feminist teach writing? At the risk of oversimplifying, her answer goes something like this: use collaborative writing, such as small group peer criticism; value the lack of hierarchical structure in the student-teacher relationship; be a nurturing mother who avoids conflict and taking authority; give 'women's language the power to surface and replace men's language' (Stanger 1987:42).

As my critique of voice in chapter 2 would suggest, I find the equation of voice with power, of process pedagogy with feminist pedagogy naïve, even dangerous. Given the many critiques that have been made of process pedagogies since 1987 (see chapter 1) and of the ways texts produced in and through them may work to enforce the gender order, such approaches to experience require serious revision. This is a challenge taken up by Jarrat (1991) in her argument for a more rhetorical feminist composition. For Jarratt the expressivist focus on student experiences is only a starting point for feminist pedagogy; it is also crucial, she argues, that feminist compositionists help 'their students learn how to argue about public issues—making the turn from the personal back out to the public' (Jarratt 1991:121).

> My hopes are pinned on composition courses whose instructors help their students to locate personal experiences in historical and social contexts . . . in which students argue about the ethical implications of discourse on a wide range of subjects and, in so doing, come to identify their personal interests with others, understand those interests as implicated in a larger communal setting, and advance them in a public voice. (Jarratt 1991:121)

Similar concerns are raised by Julie McLeod (1999) in the context of women's studies, particularly the danger of a too exclusive focus on genres of experience and a consequent devaluing of critique. In her discussion of the place of experience in the women's studies and feminist classroom, McLeod identifies the transformative possibilities—the 'desire to hear and cultivate women's voices and to create a collaborative and participatory learning environment which is personally enriching and transformative' (1999:524)—as central tenets of feminist pedagogy. While acknowledging the historical importance of these goals, she also articulates her own discomfort with extravagant 'life-changing' claims made for feminist pedagogies, where heartfelt experiences are valorised as the hallmark of a successful women's studies classroom.

She argues that an overvaluing of the transformative experience has led to a devaluing of content knowledge and a reluctance to engage critically with questions of what constitutes the changing and contested curriculum of the disciplinary field of women's studies. The danger is that the personal can become 'a substitute for reading and thinking and extending understandings—for thinking beyond the self—because it privileges real personal experience over other forms of knowledge' (McLeod 1999:524).

These are important arguments. Critique is as important
to the feminist project as celebrating experience. Like McLeod
and Jarratt, I want my students to take a rigorous critical
stance on the experience they write about. The critical approach to autobiography I have outlined in this chapter is
challenging and if Karina and Alice are any measure, at times
frightening. The verb phrases used by Alice suggest hard
labour—*resurrected, ripped it out, worked it, produced it*,
and agency—*moving in, giving shape.*

In placing a high priority on the personal, then, I am
arguing for a stance to experience that is less humanistic,
less essentialised, less confessional than that practiced in
some sites of feminist pedagogy. Informed by poststructuralist
notions of narrative and fiction, it is an approach that does
not regard the experience written about—or the voice in which
it is expressed—as an inner truth which needs to be cher-
ished by a nurturing mother–writing teacher. What it does do
is challenge students to create their own hybrid fictions.

This is not a simple matter of rejecting genres such as
argument because they are perceived to be male and oppressive to women; nor of valorising a female mode of writing
which uses the personal to replace the theoretical. The challenge, rather, is to help students theorise experience by disrupting the cultural conventions of a wide variety of genres
and create new discursive positions. These, in turn, have
effects on the writer and reader as well as the institutions in
which they are written.

> To contest any fiction is to locate oneself deliber-
> ately in other fictions, to see how these fictions
> were made, to take pleasure in the crossing of bound-
> aries, the mixing of genres, the making of other
> subjects—not as an apolitical or romanticised hedo-
> nism or irresponsible pluralism—but in order to be
> able to see and to speak from a number of positions
> at once, in order to be able to understand and to
> intervene *more* not less. (Threadgold 1992:5)

CHAPTER SEVEN

The Politics of the Personal:
New Metaphors, New Practices

———————————❖———————————

Metaphors of spatiality have been central to the conception
of writing I have developed in this book. The act of writing
creates a space of representation where the personal is written and rewritten, but not confused with 'the person'. The
writing teacher creates a pedagogic space, where she works
with writers to shape both text and the writer's subjectivity.
A politics of space foregrounds the location and locatedness
of the writer, as well as the need to create distance between
the writer and the experience written about, so that experience itself is relocated in other spaces—political, social, cultural—rather than understood simply as the province of the
private and individual.

Within this space, I have brought together diverse bodies
of knowledge, including recent knowledges from critical discourse analysis and poststructuralist approaches to language,
to experiment with alternate, more theorised ways of reading
and writing the personal. I have developed a critical writing
pedagogy though four teaching case studies: with older women
in adult community settings, with a high school writer failing English, with undergraduate students learning to teach
writing, and graduate students examining issues of language
and gender. This focus on different educational sites (secondary, undergraduate, graduate, adult/community) and differently

positioned writers has allowed me to explore a variety of ways of working critically, rather than promote a singular 'best method'.

During the past four decades the field of literacy education has been riven with debates about best methods, with each new theory and associated pedagogies promising to solve the problems of the past approach (Kamler 1998; Luke 1998). In Australia, we have seen volatile debates about the best way to teach writing, with a number of different paradigms, such as process and genre approaches, struggling for dominance—with profound effects on curriculum development, policy statements, inservice provision and the funding of research (Comber 1996).

Rather than getting locked into debates over which way is *the* best way to teach writing, Freebody and Luke (1990) argue that a more productive question is which aspects of literacies are offered by various approaches? It is not that a particular approach is necessarily best, but that each 'displays and emphasises particular forms of literacy, such that no single one will, of itself, fully enable students to use texts effectively, in their own individual and collective interests, across a range of discourses, texts and tasks' (1990:7–8).

My approach in this book has highlighted, instead, the importance of working with a multiplicity of frameworks (process, genre, linguistic, critical discourse analytic, poststructuralist feminist) rather than one. Through a close textual analysis of critical moments in my own history as teacher, researcher, writer and student, I have sought to identify strengths and weaknesses of various approaches, as well as gaps and silences. Most importantly, I have highlighted the problem of locating oneself as a teacher of writing in one paradigm only. I have demonstrated the richness to be gained by incorporating perspectives of more recent positions, particularly critical discourse analysis and feminist poststructuralism, to extend and rewrite the earlier work.

A number of understandings have been critical to this rewriting, in particular the need to develop different notions of the person and more politicised purposes for personal writing, than those usually associated with either process or genre approaches. To produce writing that does not essentialise the writer's individual voice has meant challenging the dominant conception of the student writer as a rational, coherent and unitary individual and her writing as a neutral vehicle for expressing the thoughts and emotions of a unique individual consciousness. It has meant working with a post-structuralist notion of self as constituted in and through discursive practices. It has also meant framing personal writing as a political project rather than a site of authenticity, emotion and true feelings and refashioning the writing workshop as a space for a politics of representation—for counter-narrative work which challenges dominant representations and storylines.

Of course, the process of developing these understandings has itself involved a journey of relocation. The reader will recall that at the end of chapter 1, we left our writing teacher, 'Till Death Do Us Part' text in one hand, 'Girls into Concrete' in the other, looking to the future, in search of a new theoretical framework. Since that time she has learned a great deal. Having traversed the years and pages that make up this book, having located and relocated herself in four very different teaching contexts, what can she now say with certainty? Exactly what is this critical writing pedagogy she would propose?

A CONTEXT–SPECIFIC CASE STUDY APPROACH

The writer has worked hard to assert the importance of a critical writing pedagogy—not as a new method—but as a politicised frame which can help teachers think differently about teaching writing and reflect on *what* it is students are learning to write, what they *do* with that writing and what that writing *does* to them and their world.

Her concern has been *not* to construct a book of advice or promote a view of writing that is prescriptive. This is not a textbook of *the* way to teach the personal. Despite years of writing scholarship and truckloads of books promoting their way of teaching writing as THE BEST—THE ONLY—THE NEWEST—

she believes there is no single truth. All stories, including stories of pedagogy, are partial; they are particular rather than general, they represent a perspective, a way of seeing that is complex and multifaceted, rather than universal.

This is inevitable as all writing involves a politics of selection. The case studies enumerated in this book, for example, construct omissions and absences as well as inclusions. They focus primarily on gender, rather than class or race because of the contexts and disciplines in which the writer has been located—both theoretically and spatially. Nevertheless, the writer believes the pedagogy enumerated here has space for making such concerns central, including the multiplicity of ways various technologies might reshape text and subjectivity. But that remains the work of another volume and other writers.

Here the writer has refused the grand narrative of teaching writing and opted instead for a context–specific case study approach. The four case studies cross disciplinary boundaries— teacher education, composition, English, women's studies, linguistics—and educational boundaries—primary, secondary, undergraduate, postgraduate, adult. They engage a multiplicity of literacies—critical literacy, adult literacy, language arts, English literacy, genre literacy, literary literacy—and combine a variety of theoretical frameworks that do not often go together in the teaching of writing. This is their strength.

Readers can engage with the specificity and locality of the writing produced in each case and read these against their own contexts for commonalities and differences. They can bring a critical lens to the particular strategies and teaching dilemmas that arise in each chapter, selecting those that are appropriate, rejecting others, considering how these might be written differently. It is the writer's hope that these strategies prompt the reader to develop other critical writing practices (appropriate for their own locations) and a greater self-consciousness about how such practices affect both the writer's subjectivity and the text she writes; how the stories support, undermine and struggle with other stories.

This case study approach also allows readers to employ a multiplicity of reading practices, both within and across educational and disciplinary boundaries. Teachers of women's studies, for example, may find chapter 6 most relevant for the autobiographical textwork on language and gender; language and literacy teacher educators may find chapter 5 compelling for the discourse analytic work with preservice teachers; teachers of adult literacy, nursing or community medicine may read chapter 3 for the counternarrative work in community settings and its impact on the well-being of older women; high school English and remedial literacy teachers may find chapter 4 useful for strategies of teaching argument that help students meet testing and curriculum requirements.

It is also possible, however, to read across the chapters for genre–specific strategies. The focus in chapter 4 on teaching Sasha argument, for example, might be read as a starting point for teaching argument in disciplines other than English; the claywork strategies and linguistic metalanguage may be refashioned for working with university undergraduates in composition, education or other discipline–specific sites. Those interested in argument, however, might also read across to chapter 5 for other linguistic strategies, such as 'the coloured underlines' or 'do you buy it' and reimagine how these might be transformed for use in elementary classrooms.

The case studies also highlight strategies for disrupting genres, and it is possible to read these for ways of questioning dominant discourses and cultural conventions. So, teachers interested in counternarrative work, autobiography as cultural criticism or authoethnography may read chapter 1 for a particular modelling of cross–genre writing, which introduces narratives of lived experience into the academic essay, or chapter 6 for disruptive ways of writing research (such as the transcript poem) and borrowing techniques from other genres to theorise the construction of gendered subjectivities. While the teaching contexts examined in this book have primarily focused on questions of gender, teachers in composition, cultural studies, postcolonial studies or education may use these as a starting point to imagine other autoethnographic writing on the construction of race, class, ethnicity, generation, sexuality and the intersections between these.

Other mappings are possible. The combinations and re-combinations are endless, depending on the teacher's local and specific teaching needs and the needs of her students. The aim has been to create multiple spaces for teacher agency and experimentation with different genres, different purposes, differently located subjects. A number of features of this pedagogy, however, can be teased out from the specificity of each case, and it is to these I now turn.

FROM VOICE TO STORY

A key feature of this pedagogy has been the decision to use story rather than voice as a metaphor of the personal. This may or may not be a popular move, but a recent publication by Yancey (1994) confirms the value of doing so. In this collection, Yancey brings together a number of writing teachers, located within the disciplinary site of composition, to engage with voice as 'one of the most frequently used metaphors employed in rhetoric and composition' (1994:xx). This project is an important one in mapping a multiplicity of uses of the term to see what these enable and constrain 'theoretically, personally, conventionally, pedagogically, culturally, ideologically, technologically' (1994:xx). Surprisingly, however, the volume lacks self-consciousness about a variety of political critiques outside composition (and outside progressive student–centred paradigms), such as those rehearsed in chapter 2 from critical and feminist post-structuralist positions. In the end, what seems to be celebrated is multiplicity, leaving the metaphor of voice intact without calling it into question.

My purposes here are different and more critical—to argue for a notion of the personal which is not simply equated with voice. While chapter 2 acknowledges the importance of recent poststructural efforts to retheorise voice as multiple, situated and partial, even these critiques raise serious questions about the adequacy of the term and its usefulness for a relocation of personal writing within the social, cultural and political domains.

I have opted instead for the construct of narrative because it allows for a more textual orientation than voice, a closer attention to text and textuality, a different treatment of the person (who writes) and the personal (the text they write). Metaphors of textuality, I argue, are more productive for a critical writing pedagogy because they foreground practices of *representation, labour and analysis.*

With regard to *representation,* a clearer separation can be made between the writer's life and the experience she is writing about. What the writer produces is a text, a story, that comes from her but is *not* her. The construct 'story' offers a strong theoretical basis for separating life from text, the personal experience from its representation on the page, as Summerfield (1994) argues in the context of college composition.

> as teachers . . . we can usefully distinguish the life from the text, the events being represented, the 'what happened,' from the procedures for representing what happened—the textual options. We ask students, then for their texts, not their lives. The distinction is crucial: the discourse is not the event. It is not real life. To distinguish event from discourse is to . . . foreground in the classroom, questions about how and why we remember, how writing transforms memory, and how discourse arises out of the writing or telling situation. (Summerfield 1994:183)

The construct of narrative allows teachers to foreground all writing as a representation, not *the* truth but *a* version, a fiction; it then becomes possible to ask writerly questions about the personal without critiquing the writer's life; to ask how experience is portrayed, which aspects are included, excluded, emphasised, metaphored and with what effects.

With regard to *labour,* metaphors of textuality make the labour of the writer more visible and less naturalised than metaphors of voice. If stories are constructed, if they are made rather than found, they ostensibly can be remade and rewritten. Voice, by contrast, emphasises natural and authentic expression which is effortless—just like speaking—something you have rather than learn. The implication is that some students have it, some don't; some can find it, some can't. Like magic.

The construct of narrative, by contrast, allows the teacher to foreground the craft of writing as social and textual construction, a deliberate making. It then becomes possible to make such practices the object of overt instruction, much as I did in my claywork with Sasha in chapter 4. This demands a more active engagement with the student on the page, not through teacherly margin notes or a running monologue at the front of the classroom, but by showing, by moving spatially, by taking the student text apart and putting it back together. The aim is to create greater agency for the writer and reposition her as a textworker, someone who can work actively and consciously (first with more—later with less assistance) to shape the body of a text.

Finally, with regard to *analysis*, metaphors of textuality foreground the power of stories as interpretative resources for dealing with the everyday world and taking ourselves up within the cultural storylines available to us. They frame the personal as learned cultural practice, able to be analysed in relation to cultural contexts of production, rather than simply celebrated or surveilled for the right/wrong voice.

I have highlighted the importance of linguistics in this analytic work, in particular systemic functional linguistics (Halliday 1985), for examining the ways in which discourses speak in and through the writer as she writes the personal onto the (never neutral) page. While linguistics can be a powerful tool for the study of power and ideology in everyday texts, the work in chapter 5 confirms the need to use linguistics in conjunction with socially critical theories such as poststructuralism and feminisms. Without these, we are in danger of giving undue attention to linguistic form and technologies of analysis at the expense of questioning relations of power.

MULTIPLE PERSPECTIVES, MULTIPLE PRACTICES

A major strength of this critical writing pedagogy is its use of multiple frameworks (process, genre, systemic linguistic, critical discourse analytic, poststructuralist feminist) for working with the personal. This commitment to multiplicity is not simply a poststructural celebration of indeterminacy or an untheorised eclecticism, a bag of best writing tricks developed over the past ten years. Rather it allows for a variety of intersections and selections by teachers in recognition of the fact that literacy practices

> constitute, and are constituted by, the economic, cultural and political contexts in which they occur. "Literacies" and literacy education, then, are by definition always local and always particular, always working in concert with issues of identity, power and access in particular institutions, communities and cultures. (Farrell *et al.* 1995:1)

The four case studies in this book have demonstrated at least four kinds of literacy practices for working in particular institutional contexts:

1. Writing process practices for crafting and revising text
2. Genre–based practices for developing text structure
3. Linguistic practices for thematising, modalising, nominalising and building authority in text
4. Poststructuralist practices for examining questions of subjectivity, power and the ways in which texts are produced.

As a writing teacher, it is the way these practices intersect that is of interest to me. I do not promote one at the

expense of the other but use them in combination—
foregrounding some, backgrounding others—and incorporating these within a larger set of political purposes that treat
writing as social action.

In my work with older women in chapter 3, for example,
poststructuralist feminist understandings of positioning and
representation were used to develop new conference questions on absence and contradiction and to experiment with
visual framing exercises, where multiple narratives are constructed from the same visual image. In the language, gender and education course in chapter 6, such understandings
became the actual focus of analysis as students read poststructural theory, wrote a cultural autobiography and critically reflected on the problems of that textual making. In
both contexts the purposes for writing were political; in the
former, to counter dominant discourses of ageing by writing
counternarratives; in the latter, to examine the construction of gendered subjectivities and rewrite new positions
from which to speak as women. But the critical writing
practices enacted in each context used similar understandings differently.

This occurred as well with the development of linguistic
knowledge in chapters 4 and 5. In my work with Sasha , a
linguistic metalanguage was developed in conjunction with
poststructuralist notions of power and subjectivity. The aim
was not to make Sasha a linguist but to develop multiple
resources for asserting authority in life and text in order to
improve her argumentative writing. In my work with Tammi,
Karen, Bronwyn and David, the linguistic work was more
self-conscious and itself an object of critique as students
struggled with what it meant to use linguistics critically. In
chapters 3 and 6, by contrast, linguistics was not used at all
to help older women and Master's students disrupt cultural
conventions of narrative. Such flexibility—I would argue—
making particular knowledges explicit, inexplicit or absent,
positions teachers well to develop new ways of working with
the personal in particular 'institutions, communities, and
cultures' (Farrell *et al.* 1995:1).

WRITING AS A DESIGN FOR SUBJECTIVITY AND TEXT

A further feature of this critical writing pedagogy is its view of the writing workshop as a pedagogic space for designing both text and subjectivity. Taking up Kress' (1996) social semiotic theory of representation allows the teacher to understand the intimate and reciprocal relationship between the forms of representation and the forms of subjectivity produced.

The case studies demonstrate a variety of strategies for extending the cultural resources of the writer and challenging the forms of representation available to her. We have seen writers experiment with telling facts in order to write with greater specificity; with writing in the third person, as if the story were about someone else; with reading discourses and absences in their own texts or taking texts apart to see how they are nominalised, thematised, modalised, made. Each of these strategies of rewriting and analysis have the power to remake text differently; they also have the power to remake self and reposition writers with greater agency.

In chapter 2, I argue that writing the personal can transform the writer's subjectivity but caution against notions of transformation that are too grand, too therapeutic, too located in universal goals of liberation and social change. The stories presented in this book have been transformative for the writers—to greater and lesser degrees. For some writers a transformed subjectivity manifested physically as in the lifting of dark rings from Bella's eyes or the commencement of Karina's menstruation following the writing of her cultural autobiography. For other writers, transformation involved learning to assert themselves more powerfully in public spaces, as in Rowena's triumphant march out of the hospital or Sasha's ability to make authoritative claims about vegetarianism; still others confronted unspeakable fears semiotically, as did Alice in her textual retaliation against her Malaysian family and subsequent release from guilt and pain.

It is important to stress that such writing was not only crafted to produce better text, but to produce new practices that serve the writer's life purposes and challenge the communities in which she lives. It seems to me that historically, we have focused on textwork but ignored the material and bodily effects of that writing. If, however, teachers understand that it is through the processes of writing that writers reconstruct and renegotiate subjectivity, then we have to think differently and more critically about the spaces where we teach writing.

WRITING AS A POLITICAL PROJECT IN SCHOOLS AND COMMUNITIES

A final feature of this critical writing pedagogy is its commitment to a political understanding of writing. The four case studies in this book demonstrate that relocating the personal is never simply about technique or strategy but always also about power and social action. In a recent article with Barbara Comber (Comber and Kamler 1997), we argue that even when teachers avoid explicitly political work in their literacy lessons—even when they treat particular kinds of information and cultural forms as though they are neutral and unproblematic, their teaching still has political effects on learners, texts and possible social futures.

The times in which we live make it more important than ever for teachers of writing to look beyond the classroom, beyond method, beyond debates about what might be the right or wrong way to teach writing. It's not that these debates are not central to our work as teachers, but that they keep our attention fixed too narrowly on method (Luke 1998) and allow us as a profession to neglect an understanding of the relationship between literacy and broader social and cultural change.

I hold onto the optimistic view that critical approaches to writing can lead to agency for writers and the possible negotiation of social justice in particular school communities; conversely, that we are in danger of losing critical agendas for educational reform if our focus remains too narrowly fixed on outcomes and methods. I hold onto that optimism for local change, even while acknowledging the impossibility of educational reform on a large scale.

I began this book by asking what it might mean to re-locate the personal in larger social and political contexts. I have told a number of stories, both to illustrate what such personal writing might look like and to examine the effects of teaching the personal as an embodied social and political act. As I move to the end of this book, however, there is one story that remains to be told—a story that returns me to the beginning, to politics, critique and a final tale of relocation.

I have called the story Raymond Crosses the Street. It is a genesis narrative which traces my commitment to a poli-tics of representation back to New Jersey in 1963—to a teacher named Jo McFarlane and a student named Raymond, who first politicized my understanding of writing. This story re-mains deeply written into my body, rediscovered during the process of writing this book, serving now as its beginning and its end. It is a story which reminds us that critical spaces can make a difference to the lives of students and that with-out teacher intervention, stories which relocate the personal may never be told.

RAYMOND CROSSES THE STREET: NEW JERSEY 1963

We are in year 10 and our English teacher is Jo McFarlane, a Harvard graduate with a Master's de-gree, a reputation as a radical teacher and a tough marker. She constructs a performance of teaching which relocates my desire to learn. The narrative Jo McFarlane tells about herself on the first day of school remains written in my body because it is such a transgressive text for the times. She tells us her first name (unheard of) and makes reference to a personal life outside the classroom (she is divorced). We imagine her as a promiscuous lover of hand-some men, men as intensely intellectual and exciting as she. As our discourses are entirely heterosexist in those days, it never occurs to us to imagine a lesbian lover.

Jo McFarlane wears straight skirts and sits on the edge of our desks as she engages us in conversation. She sets ground rules about how many texts we need to read and write during the year and sets deadlines which we must learn to meet. She invites us to join her in learning spaces outside the classroom , poetry readings at the 92nd Street Y by Howard Nemerov and Gregory Corso and off-broadway productions by Pinter and Albee. She reads us novels, essays, reviews from the *New York Times Review of Books* . She talks of theatre and art at MOMA and the MET. She tells us she will leave her classroom open at lunch time so we can sit, talk, eat—sometimes she will be there, sometimes not.

The freedom Jo McFarlane offers infuses reading and writing with a pleasure I have never before experienced. She requires that we write four pieces each semester, ungraded. Pass/Fail only. She reads aloud the most interesting student writing and teaches from a wide variety of models. The assignment I remember is one where she suggests we write about an experience without telling what the larger scene is. Just use the details she says. (Are these the same telling facts that, thirty years later, I will urge writers to use in their texts of the everyday?)

I struggle for weeks to capture on paper an experience I have with my mother in the New York subway. I am amazed that I like to do this writing. It doesn't seem hard. My mother and I are standing on the platform as a blind man approaches the train, clicking his cane. Unexpectedly, his foot slips into the space between the platform and the train—a slip that can pull him to his death. His foot slips again and again into that dark space and my stomach lurches. Suddenly someone grabs his arm and releases his foot. He gets onto the train, safe, and the doors shut. The moment passes, the platform is empty and I experience the first pleasure I have ever experienced writing. It is seductive and sweet.

I do not even ask my mother for help. I am ecstatic when my paper is read out loud to the whole class.

But the most radical thing Jo McFarlane does is open her classroom at lunchtime. I later learn this is not just an invitation to eat. This is a political space in a school that mandates students be located in the cafeteria and gym at lunchtime. McFarlane teaches the highest and lowest streamed tracks of English. The community in which we live is predominantly Jewish with Black and Italian families the minority. It is a demarcated space—those with money live on the hill, those without in the village. McFarlane names the demarcation as problematic. She says the tracking system ensures we will never be in the same classes and never have cause to speak to or listen to one another. This troubles her. So she opens her room for us to meet.

I go to this room. It is my first act of defiance, of boundary crossing. And in this room I become friends with 'the boys' who talk tough and irreverently. In this room we tell stories. But it is Raymond's story that I remember thirty-three years later.

Raymond tells what it's like to stand at the traffic lights on Walnut Street waiting to cross the street. Raymond is walking along Walnut Street and just as he reaches the corner the light turns red. So he stops. And in the mini-split second it takes to look up at the Cadillac, stopped at the lights, he sees it. The right hand of the white man in the cadillac reaches for the button and presses it down. Raymond is a six-foot-tall African American boy. He is tall, lanky and goofy the way high school boy bodies were in 1963. He's standing at the lights. He stops. The car stops. The hand moves to the button.

I see this motion again and again—a black man at a red light—a Cadillac at the corner—a hand to the button to protect the precious white cargo inside. Raymond realises in that instant that they fear him. They don't know him, he isn't dangerous-looking. The white people in the car are afraid because he is black. He cannot compute that he is dangerous, but in that split second move he is devastated.

The room is silenced by his narrative. We are crying. But I am also inside the car. I am sitting in the back seat as we drive through downtown Newark. The streets are empty. We approach the red light. There are two black men standing on the corner of Vauxhall Road. My father says nothing but he moves his hand to the button and centrally locks us in. These are the days before car hijackings when people do not yet force motorists out of their cars at gunpoint. Yet this is also a Newark that will explode in 1968 with race riots. I am glad to be locked in. The two black men cross the street, we watch them. Then the light turns green and our car moves on, relieved.

Raymond's telling, however, forces me out of the backseat. His story propels me to the corner where, now relocated beside him, I watch the family from the outside—through the tinted glass windows of the Cadillac. I see the father's white hand reach out again and again to the button—pushing the button down and down and down to centrally lock the family into a General Motors illusion of safety.

'Man,' Raymond says, 'who could be afraid of me?'

That's right. Who? I remain silent, unwilling to confess anything. Yet Raymond's narrative forces a relocation and in that relocation a space for critique opens that did not exist before his telling. I am mortified by my complicity in constructing his otherness. My embarrassment, my apology was never spoken but I continued to go to the room. The room that set me at odds with my father, the room where I first learned there are discourses for denaturalising the everyday practices of race and class. And so it is that English teaching, writing, critique and the personal come together in that moment in ways that will take me years to unravel and build upon.

Bibliography

Atwell, N. (1987) *In the Middle: Writing, Reading, and Learning with Adolescents*. Portsmouth, NH: Heinemann.

Bartholomae, D. (1985) 'Inventing the University.' In M. Rose (ed.), *When a Writer Can't Write: Writer's Block and Other Composing Process Problems*. New York: Guildford, 134–165.

Bourdieu, P. (1990) *The Logic of Practice*. Trans. R. Nice. Cambridge: Polity Press.

Britton, J., Burgess, T., Martin, N., McLeod, A. and Rosen, H. (1975) *The Development of Writing Abilities 11–18*. London: Macmillan.

Brodkey, L. (1992) 'Articulating Poststructural Theory in Research on Literacy'. In R. Beach, J.L. Green, M.L. Kamil and T. Shanahan (eds), *Multidisciplinary Perspectives on Literacy Research*. Urbana, ILL: *National Council on Research in English* and *National Council of Teachers of English*.

———. (1994) 'Writing on the Bias'. *College English* 56, 527–47.

———. (1996a) *Writing Permitted in Designated Areas Only*. Minneapolis: University of Minnesota Press.

———. (1996b) 'I Site'. *Open Letter* 6 (2), 17–30.

Calkins, L. (1986) *The Art of Teaching Writing*. Porstmouth, NH: Heinemann.

Cameron, D. (1992) *Feminism and Linguistic Theory*, 2nd ed. London: Macmillan.

Caywood, C.L. and Overing, G.R. (1987) *Teaching Writing: Pedagogy, Gender and Equity*. Albany, NY: State University of New York Press.

Christie, F. (1984) 'Young Children's Writing Development: The Relationship of Written Genres to Curriculum Genres'. In

B. Bartlett and J. Carr (eds.), *Language in Education Conference: A Report of Proceedings*, Brisbane: Mr Gravatt College of Advanced Education, 41–69.

———. (1986) 'The Construction of Knowledge in the Junior Primary School. *Language in Education Conference, Language and Socialisation: Home and School*, Sydney: Macquarie University.

———. (1989) *Writing in Schools: Study Guide*. Geelong, Victoria: Deakin University Press.

———. (1990) *Literacy for a Changing World*. Melbourne, Victoria: Australian Council for Educational Research.

———, Gray, P. Gray, B., Macken, M., Martin, J. and Rothery, J. (1990) *Language: A Resource for Meaning*. Sydney: Harcourt Brace Jovanovich.

Clark, R. and Ivanic, R. (1997) *The Politics of Writing*. London: Routledge.

Clifford, J. and Schlib, J. (eds) (1994) 'Introduction'. *Writing Theory and Critical Theory*. New York: Modern Language Association.

Comber, B. (1993) 'Classroom Explorations in Critical Literacy'. *Australian Journal of Language and Literacy* 16 (1), 73–83.

———. (1994) 'Critical Literacy: An Introduction to Australian Debates and Perspectives'. *Journal of Curriculum Studies* 26 (6), 655–68.

———. (1996) *The Discursive Construction of Literacy in a Disadvantaged School*. Unpublished PhD Thesis, James Cook University of North Queensland.

——— and Kamler, B. (1997) 'Critical Literacies: Politicising the Language Classroom'. *Interpretations, Special Issue Critical Literacies* 30 (1), 30–53.

——— and Simpson, A. (1995) *Reading Cereal Boxes: Analysing Everyday Texts*. Adelaide: Department for Education and Children's Services.

Davies, B. (1992) 'Women's Subjectivity and Feminist Stories'. In C. Ellis and M. Flahert (eds.), *Research on Subjectivity: Windows on Lived Experience*. Newbury Park, CA: Sage, 55–76.

———. (1994) *Poststructuralist Theory and Classroom Practice*. Geelong, Victoria: Deakin University Press.

Delpit, L. (1988) 'The Silenced Dialogue: Power and Pedagogy in Educating Other People's Children'. *Harvard Educational Review* 58 (3), 280–98.

Derewianka, B. (1990) *Exploring How Texts Work*. Sydney: Primary English Teaching Association.

Disadvantaged Schools Program. (1988) *Teaching Factual Writing: A Genre Based Approach*. Sydney: Metropolitan East Region

Dixon, K. (1995) 'Gendering the "Personal" '. *College Composition and Communication* 46 (2), 255–75.

Dressman, M. (1993) 'Lionizing Lone Wolves: The Cultural Romantics of Literacy Workshops'. *Curriculum Inquiry* 23, 245–63.

Dyson, A.H. (1992) 'The Case of the Singing Scientist'. *Written Communication* 9 (1), 3–47.

Eggins, S., Martin, J.R. and Wignell, P. (eds.) (1987) *Working Papers in Linguistics, Writing Project Report 5*. Department of Linguistics, University of Sydney, 25–65.

Elbow, P. (1994) 'What Do We Mean When We Talk about Voice in Texts?' In K.B. Yancey (ed.), *Voices on Voice*. Urbana, IL: National Council of Teachers of English, 1–35.

Ellsworth, E. (1992) 'Why Doesn't This Feel Empowering? Working Through the Repressive Myths of Critical Pedagogy'. In C. Luke and J. Gore (eds.), *Feminisms and Critical Pedagogy*. London: Routledge, 90–119.

Faigley, L. (1994) *Fragments of Rationality: Postmodernity and the Subject of Composition*. Pittsburgh: University of Pittsburgh Press.

Fairclough, N. (1992) *Discourse and Social Change*. Cambridge: Polity Press.

———. (1995) *Critical Discourse Analysis*. London: Longman.

Farrell, L. (1998) 'Back to the Future: School Examinations, Fairness and the Question of Identity'. *Australian Educational Researcher* 25 (6), 1–17.

———, Luke, A., Shore, S. and Waring, W. (1995) 'Critical Literacy: Cultural Action and Textual Practices'. *Open Letter* 6 (1), 1–4.

Farrell, L., Kamler, B., and Threadgold, T. (2000) 'Telling Tales out of School: Women and Literacy in New Times'. *Studies in the Education of Adults* 32 (1), 78–93.

Featherstone, M. and Hepworth, M. (1991) 'The Mask of Ageing and the Post Modern Life Course'. In M. Featherstone, M. Hepworth and B.S. Turner (eds.), *The Body Social Process and Cultural Theory Condition*. London: Sage, 371–404.

Feldman, S., Kamler, B. and Threadgold, T. (1998) 'Women's Stories of Action and Reflection: Counternarratives of Ageing'. Paper presented at the International Sociology Conference, Montreal, 26 July–1 August.

Flynn, E. (1991) 'Composition Studies from a Feminist Perspective'. In R. Bullock and J.H. Trimbur (eds.), *The Politics of Writing Instruction: Postsecondary*. Portsmouth, NH: Boynton Cook.

Foucault, M. (1979) *Discipline and Punish*. New York: Harper.

———. (1988) 'The Ethic of Care for the Self as a Practice of Freedom' (interview conducted by Raul Fornet-Betancourt, Helmut Becker, Alfredo Gomez-Muller). Translated by J.D. Gauthier, S.J. In J. Bernauer and D. Rasmussen (eds.), *The Final Foucault*. Cambridge: MIT Press, 1–20.

———. (1997) 'Writing the Self'. In A. Davidson (ed.), *Foucault and His Interlocutors*. Chicago: University of Chicago Press, 234–47.

Fowler, R. and Kress, G. (1979) 'Critical Linguistics'. In R. Fowler, R. Hodge, G. Kress and T. Trew (eds.), *Language and Control*. London: Routledge, 185–213.

Freebody, P. and Luke, A. (1990) ' "Literacies" Programs: Debates and Demands in Cultural Context'. *Prospect: The Journal of Adult Migrant Education Programs* 5 (3), 7–16.

Freebody, Luke and Gilbert, P. (1991) 'Reading Positions and Practices in the Classroom'. *Curriculum Inquiry* 21 (4), 435–57.

Freedman, A. and Medway, P. (eds.) (1995a) *Genre and the New Rhetoric*. London: Falmer Press.

———. (eds.) (1995b) *Learning and Teaching Genre*. Portsmouth, NH: Heinemann.

——— and Richardson, P. (1998) 'Literacy and Genre'. In N. Hornberger and D. Corson (eds.), *Encyclopedia of Language and Education. Knowledge about Language*, Chapter 17, Volume 6. Dordrecht/Boston/London: Kluwer Academic, 139–149.

Freedman, D.P. (1992) *An Alchemy of Genres: Cross-Genre Writing by American Feminist Poet-Critics*. Charlottesville: University Press of Virginia.

Freire, P. (1970) *Pedagogy of the Oppressed*. New York: Continuum.

————. (1985). *The Politics of Education: Culture, Power and Liberation*. South Hadley: Bergin and Garvey.

Fuss, D. (1989) *Essentially Speaking: Feminism, Nature and Difference*. New York: Routledge.

Gilbert, P. (1989) *Writing, Schooling and Deconstruction*. London: Routledge.

————. (1990) 'Authorizing Disadvantage: Authorship and Creativity in the Language Classroom'. In F. Christie (ed.), *Literacy for a Changing World*. Melbourne: Australian Council for Educational Research, 54–78.

————. (1993a) *Gender Stories and the Language Classroom*. Geelong, Victoria: Deakin University Press.

————. (1993b) '(Sub)versions: Using Sexist Language Practices to Explore Critical Literacy'. *Australian Journal of Language and Literacy* 16 (4), 323–32.

Giroux, H. (1988) 'Literacy and the Pedagogy of Voice and Political Empowerment'. *Educational Theory* 38 (1), 61–75.

———— and McLaren, P.L. (eds.). (1989) *Critical Pedagogy, the State, and Cultural Struggle*. Albany, NY: State University of New York Press.

Golebiowski, Z. and Borland, H. (1997) *Academic Communication across Disciplines and Cultures: Selected Proceedings of the First National Conference on Tertiary Literacy, Research and Practice*. Melbourne: Victoria University of Technology.

Graves, D. (1983) *Writing: Teachers and Children at Work*. Porstmouth, NH: Heinemann.

Green, B. (1987) 'Gender, Genre and Writing Pedagogy'. In I. Reid (ed.), *The Place of Genre in Learning: Current Debates*. Geelong, Victoria: Deakin University Press, 83–90.

————, Hodgens, J. and Luke, A. (1997) 'Debating Literacy in Australia: History Lessons and Popular F(r)ictions'. *Australian Journal of Language and Literacy* 20 (1), 6–24.

Grumet, M. (1990) 'Voice: The Search for a Feminist Rhetoric for Educational Studies'. *Cambridge Journal of Education* 20 (3), 277–82.

Halliday, M.A.K. (1978) *Language as Social Semiotic*. London: Edward Arnold.

——. (1985) *Introduction to Functional Grammar*. London: Edward Arnold.

—— and Hasan, R. (1989) *Language, Context and Text: Aspects of Language in a Social-Semiotic Perspective*. Oxford: Oxford University Press. (Original work published 1985, Deakin University Press.)

—— and Martin, J. (1993) *Writing Science*. London: Falmer Press.

Hammond, J. (1990) 'Is Learning to Read and Write the Same as Learning to Speak?' In F. Christie (ed.), *Literacy for a Changing World*. Melbourne Victoria: Australian Council for Educational Research, 260–53.

Hargreaves, A. (1996) 'Revisiting Voice'. *Educational Researcher*, January–February, 12–19.

Haug, F. (ed.) (1987) *Female Sexualization: A Collective Work of Memory*. London: Verso.

Hayes, J. and Flower, L. (1980) 'Identifying the Organization of Writing Processes: An Interdisciplinary Approach'. In L. Gregg and E. Steinberg (eds.), *Cognitive Processes in Writing*. Hillsdale, NJ: Lawrence Erlbaum.

——. (1983) 'Uncovering Cognitive Processes in Writing: An Introduction to Protocol Analysis'. In P. Mosenthal, L. Tamor and S. Walmsley (eds.), *Research on Writing: Principles and Methods*. New York: Longman.

Henriques, J., Hollway, W., Urwin, C., Venn, C. and Walkerdine, V. (1984) *Changing the Subject: Psychology, Social Regulation and Subjectivity*. London: Methuen.

Hodge, R. and Kress, G. (1988) *Social Semiotics*. Cambridge: Polity Press.

Huggins, J. (1992) 'A Contemporary View of Aboriginal Women's Relationship to the White Women's Movement'. In *A Woman's Place in Australia*. Geelong, Victoria: Faculty of Humanities, Deakin University, 16–26.

Jaggar, A. (1983) *Feminist Politics and Human Nature*. Towtow, NJ: Rowman and Allenheld.

Janks, H. (ed.). (1993) *Critical Language Awareness Series*. Johannesburg: Hodder and Stoughton and Wits University Press.

———. (1997) 'Critical Discourse Analysis as a Research Tool'. In B. Kamler, B. Comber and J. Cooke (eds.), *Discourse* 18 (3) 329–42.

Jarratt, S. (1991) 'Feminism and Composition: The Case for Conflict'. In P. Harkin and J. Schlib (eds.), *Contending with Words: Composition and Rhetoric in a Postmodern Age*. New York: Modern Language Association, 105–23.

Kamler, B. (1980) 'One Child, One Teacher, One Classroom: The Story of One Piece of Writing'. *Language Arts* 57, 680–93.

———. (1981) 'One Child, One Teacher, One Classroom.' In R. D. Walshe (ed.), *Donald Graves in Australia: Children Want to Write*. Sydney: Primary English Teaching Association, 73–88.

———. (1987) 'Observations of One Child Learning to Write in Two Classroom Contexts'. In B. Kamler and C. Woods. *Two Pathways to Literacy. AATE Action Research Studies No. 2*. Canberra, Australian Capital Territory: Australian Association for the Teaching of English, 1–58.

———. (1990) *Gender and Genre in Early Writing: A Case Study of a Girl and a Boy Learning to Write*. Unpublished PhD Thesis, Geelong, Victoria: Deakin University.

———. (1993) 'Constructing Gender in the Process Writing Classroom'. *Language Arts* (70), 20–8.

———. (1994) 'Resisting Oppositions in Writing Pedagogy: What Process-Genre Debate?' *Idiom* 25 (2), 14–19.

———. (1995a) 'Grammar Wars or What do Teachers Need to Know About Grammar?' *English in Australia* 114, 3–15.

———. (1995b) 'Can Personal Writing be Empowering? Developing Critical Writing Practices in Adult Education Settings'. *Open Letter* 6 (1), 5–16.

———. (1996) 'Stories of Ageing and Loss'. *Women and Language* (Special Issue: Women and Storytelling) 19 (1), 21–6.

———. (1997) 'Text as Body, Body as Text'. In B. Kamler, B. Comber and J. Cooke (eds.), *Discourse* 18 (3) 369–88.

———. (1998) *Critical Literacy and Teachers' Work: New Discourses for New Times*. Keynote Address for Australian Language and Literacy Educators Association/Australian Association of Teaching English Joint Conference, July 5–7, Canberra, ACT.

———, Maclean, R., Reid, J. and Simpson, A. (1994) *Shaping Up Nicely: The Formation of Schoolgirls and Schoolboys in the First Month of School*. Canberra, ACT: Department of Education, Employment and Training.

——— and Feldman, S. (1995) 'Mirror Mirror on the Wall: Reflections on Ageing'. *Australian Cultural History* 13, 1–22.

——— and Comber, B. (1996) 'Critical Literacy: Not Generic—Not Developmental—Not Another Orthodoxy'. *Changing Education* 3 (1), 1–9.

——— and Threadgold, T. (1996) 'Which Thesis Did You Read?' In Z. Golebiowski and H. Borland (eds.), *Academic Communication Across Disciplines and Cultures: Selected Proceedings of the First National Conference on Tertiary Literacy: Research and Practice*, Melbourne: Victoria University of Technology 42–58.

———, Comber, B. and Cooke, J. (eds.) (1997) *Discourse* 18 (3).

———, Cousins, K., Jonas, T. and Linden, D. (1997) 'Developing a Critical Writing Pedagogy: A Discontinuous Narrative'. *English in Australia* 118 (2), 24–44.

Keith, M. and Pile, S. (1993). 'The politics of place.' In M. Keith and S. Pile (eds.), *Place and the Politics of Identity*. London and New York: Routledge, 1–21.

Kenway, J. (1991) 'Education's Feminisms'. *Gender and Education: Study Guide*. Geelong, Victoria: Deakin University, 9–82.

———. (1992) *Making Hope Practical Rather Than Despair Convincing: Some Thoughts on the Value of Post-Structuralism as a Theory of and for Feminist Change in Schools*. Paper delivered to Australian Association for Research in Education, Deakin University, Geelong, Victoria.

——— and Modra, H. (1992) 'Feminist Pedagogy and Emancipatory Possibilities'. In C. Luke and J. Gore (eds.), *Feminisms and Critical Pedagogy*. New York: Routledge, 138–66.

Kippax, S., Crawford, J., Benton, P., Gault, U. and Noesjirwan, J. (1988) 'Constructing Emotions: Weaving Meaning from Memories'. *British Journal of Sociology* 27, 19–33.

Kirsch, G. and Ritchie, J. (1995) 'Beyond the Personal: Theorizing a Politics of Location in Composition Research'. *College Composition and Communication*, 46 (1), 7–29.

Knobel, M. and Healy, A. (eds.) (1998) *Critical Literacy in the Primary Classroom*. Sydney: Primary English Teachers Association.

Kramer-Dahl, A. (1996) 'Reconsidering the Notions of Voice and Experience in Critical Pedagogy'. In C. Luke (ed.), *Feminisms and Pedagogies of Everyday Life*. Albany, NY: State University of New York Press, 242–79.

Kress, G. (1985) *Linguistic Processes in Sociocultural Practice*. Geelong, Victoria: Deakin University Press.

———. (1988) 'Language as Social Practice'. In G. Kress (ed.), *Communication and Culture*. Kensington: NSW University Press.

———. (1996) 'Writing and Learning to Write'. In D.R. Olsen and N. Torrance (eds.), *The Handbook of Human Development*. London: Blackwell.

——— and Threadgold, T. (1988) 'Towards a Social Theory of Genre'. *Southern Review* 21 (3), 215–43.

Kristeva, J. (1986) 'Women's Time'. In T. Moi (ed.), *The Kristeva Reader*. Oxford: Basil Blackwell, 187–213.

Lankshear, C. (1994) *Critical Literacy*. Occasional paper No. 3. Canberra, Australian Capital Territory: Australian Curriculum Studies Association.

Laws, G. (1995) 'Understanding Ageism: Lessons from Feminism and Postmodernism'. *The Gerontologist* 15 (1), 112–8.

Lee, A. (1993) 'Whose Geography? A Feminist-Poststructuralist Critique of Systemic 'Genre'-Based Accounts of Literacy and Curriculum'. *Social Semiotics* 3 (1), 131–56.

———. (1996) *Gender, Literacy, Curriculum: Rewriting School Geography*. London: Taylor and Francis.

———. (1997a) 'Questioning the Critical: Linguistics, Literacy and Pedagogy'. In S. Muspratt, A. Luke and P. Freebody (eds.), *Constructing Critical Literacies: Teaching and Learning Textual Practice*. Creskill, NJ: Hampton Press, 409–32.

———. (1997b) 'Working Together? Academic Literacies, Co-Production and Professional Partnerships'. *Literacy and Numeracy Studies* 7 (2), 65–84.

——— and Green, B. (1996) 'Postgraduate Studies/Postgraduate Pedagogy?' In A. Lee and B. Green (eds.), *Postgraduate Studies/ Postgraduate Pedagogy*. Broadway, New South Wales: Centre for Language and Literacy, University of Technology, Sydney, 1–8.

——— and Williams, C. (1998) *Forged in Fire: Narratives of Trauma in PhD Supervision Pedagogy*. Unpublished paper, Faculty of Education, University of Technology, Sydney.

Lensmire, T. (1998) 'Rewriting Student Voice'. *Journal of Curriculum Studies* 30 (3), 261–91.

———. (1994) 'Writing Workshop as Carnival: Reflections on an Alternative Learning Environment'. *Harvard Educational Review* 64 (4), 371–91.

Lionnet, F. (1990) 'Authoethnography: The An-Archic Style of *Dust Tracks on a Road*'. In H.L. Gates Jr. (ed.), *Reading Black, Reading Feminist*. New York: Meridian, 382–413.

Lorde, A. (1984) 'The Transformation of Silence into Language and Action'. In A. Lorde (ed.), *Sister Outsider: Essays and Speeches*. Freedom, CA: The Crossing Press, 40–44.

Luke, A. (1995) 'Text and Discourse in Education: An Introduction to Critical Discourse Analysis'. *Review of Research in Education* 21, 1–46.

———. (1994) 'Genres of Power? Literacy Education and the Production of Capital'. In R. Hasan and G. Williams (eds.), *Literacy and Society*. London: Longman.

———. (1998) 'Getting Over Method: Literacy Teaching as Work in "New Times" '. *Language Arts* 75 (4), 305–13.

———, O'Brien, J. and Comber, B. (1994) 'Making Community Texts Objects of Study'. *Australian Journal of Language and Literacy* 17 (2), 139–49.

Luke, C. (1992) 'Feminist Politics in Radical Pedagogy'. In C. Luke and J. Gore (eds.), *Feminisms and Critical Pedagogy*. London: Routledge, 25–53.

——— and Gore, J. (eds.). (1992) *Feminisms and Critical Pedagogy*. London: Routledge.

Lusted, D. (1986) 'Why Pedagogy?' *Screen* 27 (5), 2–14.

Lyotard, J.F. (1984) 'The Postmodern Condition: A Report on Knowledge'. Trans. G. Bennington and B. Massumi. *Theory and History of Literature*, vol. 10. Manchester: Manchester University Press.

Macrorie, K. (1980) *Telling Writing*, 3rd ed. Rochelle Park, NJ: Hayden.

Martin, J.R. (1984) 'Types of Writing in Infants and Primary Schools'. In L. Unsworth (ed.), *Reading, Writing, Spelling: Proceedings of the Fifth Macarthur Reading/Language Symposium*. Sydney: Macarthur Institute of Higher Education, 34–55.

———. (1985) *Factual Writing: Exploring and Challenging Social Reality*. Geelong, Victoria: Deakin University Press.

———. (1991) 'Critical Literacy: The Role of a Functional Model of Language'. *Australian Journal of Reading* 14 (2), 117–32.

———. (1992) *English Text: System and Structure*. Philadelphia: John Benjamins.

——— and Rothery, J. (1980) *Writing Project Report Number 1*. Sydney, New South Wales: Department of Linguistics, University of Sydney.

——— and Rothery, J. (1981) *Writing Project Report Number 2*. Sydney, New South Wales: Department of Linguistics, University of Sydney.

Martino, W. and Mellor, B. (1995) *Gendered Fictions*. Perth, Western Australia: Chalkface Press.

McLeod, J. (1999) ' "Experience" and the Women's Studies Curriculum'. D. Cohen, A. Lee, J. Newman, A.M. Payne, H. Scheeres, L. Shoemark and S. Tiffin (eds.). In *Winds of Change: Women and the Culture of Universities*. University of Technology, Sydney, Conference Proceedings, 2, 522–8.

———, Yates, L. and Halasa, K. (1994) 'Voice, Difference and Feminist Pedagogy'. *Curriculum Studies* 2 (2), 189–202.

Mellor, B., Patterson, A. and O'Neill, M. (1991) *Reading Fictions*. Scarborough, Western Australia: Chalkface Press.

Middleton, S. (1993) *Educating Feminists: Life Histories and Pedagogies*. New York: Teachers College Press.

Miller, C.R. (1984) 'Genre as Social Action'. *Quarterly Journal of Speech* 70, 157–78.

Miller, N. (1991) *Getting Personal: Feminist Occasions and Other Autobiographical Acts*. New York: Routledge.

Miller. S. (1990) *Textual Carnivals: The Politics of Composition*. Carbondale, IL: Southern Illinois University Press.

Moffett, J. (1968) *Teaching the Universe of Discourse: A Rationale for English Teaching Used in a Student-Centered Language Arts Curriculum*. Boston: Houghton Mifflin.

Moraga, C. and Anzaldua, G. (1983) *This Bridge Called My Back: Writings by Radical Women of Colour*. New York: Kitchen Table, Women of Colour Press.

Morgan, W. (1992) *A Post-Structuralist English Classroom: The Example of Ned Kelly*. Carlton, Victoria: Victorian Association for the Teaching of English.

Murray, D. (1982a) 'Listening to Writing'. In D. Murray *Learning by Teaching: Selected Articles on Writing and Teaching*. Montclair NJ: Boynton Cook, 53–65.

———. (1982b). 'Writing as Process: How Writing Finds Its Own Meaning'. In D. Murray *Learning by Teaching: Selected Articles on Writing and Teaching*. Montclair NJ: Boynton Cook, 17–31.

———. (1985). *A Writer Teaches Writing*. Boston: Houghton Mifflin.

Muspratt, S., Luke, A., and Freebody, P. (1997) *Constructing Critical Literacies: Teaching and Learning Textual Practice*. Cresskill, NJ: Hampton Press.

New London Group. (1996) 'A Pedagogy of Multiliteracies: Designing Social Futures'. *Harvard Educational Review* 66 (1), 60–92.

Nichols, B. (1981) *Ideology and the Image: Social Representation in the Cinema and Other Media*. Bloomington: Indiana University Press.

Ninio, A. and Bruner, J. (1978) 'The Achievement and Antecedents of Labeling'. *Journal of Child Language* 5, 1–15.

O'Brien, J. (1994a) 'Critical Literacy in an Early Childhood Classroom: A Progress Report.' *Australian Journal of Language and Literacy* (focus issue on 'Critical Literacy') 17 (1), 36–44.

———. (1994b) 'Show Mum You Love Her: Taking a New Look at Junk Mail'. *Reading* 28 (1), 43–6.

Orner, M. (1992) 'Interrupting the Calls for Student Voice in "Liberatory" Education: A Feminist Poststructuralist Perspective'. In C. Luke and J. Gore (eds.), *Feminisms and Critical Pedagogy*. London: Routledge, 74–89.

Painter, C. and Martin, J. (eds) (1986) *Writing to Mean: Teaching Genres Across the Curriculum. Occasional Papers Number 9.* Sydney: Applied Linguistics Association.

Pinar, W.F. (1997) 'Regimes of Reason and the Male Narrative Voice'. In W.G. Tierney and Y.S. Lincoln (eds.), *Representation and the Text: Reframing the Narrative Voice*. Albany, NY: State University of New York Press, 81–113.

Poynton, C. (1985) *Language and Gender: Making the Difference*. Geelong, Victoria: Deakin University Press.

———. (1990) *Address and the Semiotics of Social Relations: A Systemic Functional Account of Address Forms and Practices in Australian English*. Unpublished PhD Thesis, Sydney University.

———. (1993). 'Grammar, Language and the Social: Poststructuralism and Systemic Functional Linguistics. *Social Semiotics* 3 (1), 1–21.

Ray, R. (1996) 'A Postmodern Perspective on Feminist Gerontology'. *The Gerontologist* 36 (5), 674–80.

Reid, I. (1987) *The Place of Genre in Learning: Current Debates*. Geelong, Victoria: Centre for Studies in Literary Education, Deakin University.

Reid, J., Kamler, B., Simpson, A., and Maclean R. (1996) '"Do You See What I See": Reading a Different Classroom Scene'. *Qualitative Studies in Education* 9 (1), 87–108.

Richardson, L. (1997) *Fields of Play: Constructing an Academic Life*. New Brunswick, NJ: Rutgers University Press.

Richardson, P. (1991) 'Language as Personal Resource and as Social Construct: Competing Views of Literacy Pedagogy in Australia'. *Educational Review* 43 (2), 171–90.

Rothery, J. (1985) 'Teaching Genre in the Primary School: A Genre-Based Approach to the Development of Writing Abilities'. *Working Papers in Linguistics, No. 4*. Department of Linguistics, University of Sydney.

Schmidt, J.Z. (ed.). (1998) *Women/Writing/Teaching*. Albany, NY: State University of New York Press.

Simon, R. (1987) 'Empowerment as a Pedagogy of Possibility'. *Language Arts* 64 (4), 370–81.

———. (1992) *Teaching Against the Grain: Texts for a Pedagogy of Possibility*. New York: Bergin and Garvey.

Slevin, J.F. (1988) 'Genre Theory, Academic Discourse and Writing Within Disciplines'. In L.Z. Smith (ed.), *Audits of Meaning: A Festschrift in Honour of Ann E Berthoff*. Portsmouth, NH: Boynton Cook.

———. (1991) 'Depoliticising and Politicising Composition Studies'. In R. Bullock and J. Trimbur (eds.), *Politics of Writing Instruction: Postsecondary*. Portsmouth, NH: Boynton Cook.

Soja, E.W. (1989) *Postmodern Geographies*. London: Verso.

Spender, D. (1980) *Man Made Language*. London: Routledge and Kegan Paul.

Stanger, C. (1987) 'The Sexual Politics of the One-to-One Tutorial Approach and Collaborative Learning'. In C.L. Caywood and G.R. Overing (eds.), *Teaching Writing: Pedagogy, Gender and Equity*. Albany, NY: State University of New York Press, 19–30.

Steedman, C. (1986) *Landscape for a Good Woman: A Story of Two Lives*. London: Virago, 3–24.

Stories of Ageing Project (1999) *We're Not Nice Little Old Ladies*. Melbourne: City of Glen Eira Arts Department and International Year of the Older Person Committee.

Summerfield, J. (1994) 'Is There a Life in This Text? Reimagining Narrative'. In J. Clifford and J. Schlib (eds.), *Writing Theory and Critical Theory*. New York: Modern Language Association.

Thibault, P. (1991) *Social Semiotics as Praxis: Text, Social Meaning Making and Nabaokov's Ada*. Minneapolis: University of Minnesota Press.

Thomson, P. (1997–98) 'Narrative Issues: Key Players, Thinkers, Ideas and Texts at a Glance'. *Changing Education: A Journal for Teachers and Administrators* 4 (4) and 5 (1 & 2), 20–6.

———. (1997–98b) 'Narrative Inquiry: A Personal Exploration'. *Changing Education* 4 (4) and 5 (1 & 2), 8–12.

————. (1999) *Doing Justice: Stories of Everyday Life in Disadvantaged Schools and Neighbourhoods*. Unpublished PhD Thesis, Deakin University.

Threadgold, T. (1988) 'The Genre Debate'. *Southern Review* 21 (3), 315–30.

————. (1993) 'Performing Genre: Violence, the Making of Protected Subjects, and the Discourses of Critical Literacy and Radical Pedagogy'. *Changing English* 1 (1), 2–31.

————. (1994) 'Grammar, Genre, and the Ownership of Literacy'. *Idiom* 2, 20–8.

————. (1996) 'Everyday Life in the Academy: Postmodernist Feminisms, Generic Seductions, Rewriting and Being Heard'. In C. Luke (ed.), *Feminisms and Pedagogies of Everyday Life*. Albany, NY: State University of New York Press, 280–314.

————. (1997) *Feminist Poetics: Poeisis, Performance, Histories*. London: Routledge.

Tierney, W.G. and Lincoln, Y.S. (1997) *Representation and the Text: Reframing the Narrative Voice*. Albany, NY: State University of New York Press.

Tong, R. (1989) *Feminist Thought: A Comprehensive Introduction*. San Francisco, CA: Westview Press.

USC (University of Southern California) (1997) 'Reclaiming Voice: Ethnographic Inquiry and Qualitative Research in a Postmodern Age', June 20–22.

Van Dijk, T. (1993) *Discourse and Society* 4 (2).

Vygotsky, L. (1978) *Mind in Society: The Development of Higher Psychological Processes*. Cambridge: Harvard University Press.

Walkerdine, V. (1990) *Schoolgirl Fictions*. London: Verso.

Walsh, R.D. (ed.) (1981) *Donald Graves in Australia: Children Want to Write*. Sydney: Primary English Teaching Association.

Weedon, C. (1987) *Feminist Practice and Poststructuralist Theory*. Oxford: Basil Blackwell.

Weiler, K. (1994) 'Freire and a Feminist Pedagogy of Difference'. In P.L. McLaren and C. Lankshear (eds.), *Politics of Liberation: Paths From Freire*. London: Routledge, 12–40.

Williams, G. (1993) 'Using Systemic Grammar in Teaching Young Learners: An Introduction'. In L. Unsworth (ed.), *Literacy Learning and Teaching: Language as Social Practice in the Primary School*. Melbourne: Macmillan, 197–253.

Williams, P. (1991) *The Alchemy of Race and Rights: Diary of a Law Professor*. Cambridge: Harvard University Press, 202–15.

Yancey, K.B. (1994) 'Introduction: Definitions, Intersections, and Difference: Mapping the Landscape of Voice'. In K.B. Yancey (ed.), *Voices on Voice*. Urbana, IL: National Council of Teachers of English, vii–xxiv.

Yell, S. (1990) 'Gender, Class and Power: Text, Process and Production in Strindberg's *Miss Julie*'. In T. Threadgold and A. Cranny-Francis (eds.), *Feminine/Masculine and Representation*. Sydney: Allen and Unwin.

Index

absences, 65, 116, 180, 181
argument, 79, 83, 85–87, 90, 170,
    180
    examinations and, 94–95, 99
    feminist critique and, 170
    macrostructure of, 91
    nominalisation and, 101, 103–
        107
    relocating, 83–87
    schematic structure, 91
    spatialisation and, 95–97
    spoken and written language
        and, 105
    subjectivity and, 83, 86
    teaching of, 127–131
    text, organisation of, 93
    theme analysis and, 102
    tree paragraph schema and,
        95–100
autobiography, 155–156, 166, 170,
    175, 180
    collective, 74
    cultural critique and, 156–157
    distance learning and, 150–151
    narrative and, 144
    feminism and, 155–156, 178
    See also cultural autobiography
autoethnography, 155, 175
    defined, 4
    personal narrative and, 4

clay work, 91, 92, 95, 101, 103,
    155, 175, 178
coloured underlines, 132–134, 175
conferencing. See writing con-
    ference

coproduction, 18, 26
critical discourse analysis, 109–
    111, 113, 167, 171, 172, 175
    as frame for relocating experi-
        ence, 112–113
    defined, 112
    discourse and, 112
    making experience textual and,
        112–113
    personal writing and, 115–116,
        120
    subjectivity and, 112
    student teachers and, 119–121
    workshop practices and, 119
critical literacy
    as frame for teaching, 124–127,
        127–131, 131–134, 135
    as magic bullet, 131
    classroom practices and, 130–
        131, 179
    genre and, 92
critical pedagogy, 36–39
    critique of, 39–42, 46–47
critical writing pedagogy, 33, 34,
    82, 110, 115, 166, 171, 173
    checklists and, 130–132
    linguistic and poststructuralist
        frameworks and, 115
    multiple frameworks in, 179–180
    political understanding of
        writing and, 182
    relationship to process and
        genre, 14, 21–22, 29, 32, 33,
        35, 172, 179
    student teachers and, 110, 122,
        125–127, 135, 157

critical writing *(continued)*
    student voice and, 39–42
    See also critical discourse
       analysis; feminist poststruc-
       turalism
cross-genre writing, 155–156, 175
cultural autobiography, 137, 138–
    144, 144–148, 166

design. *See* writing, as design for
    subjectivity
discourse, 115, 119, 134, 153, 177
    defined, 112
    identity and, 85–86
    making visible, 120–121
    of the good wife, 72, 118–119
    sexist, 120–121
discourse analysis. *See* critical
    discourse analysis
disruptive genres, 156–158, 170,
    175

embodied texts, 5, 35, 114
experience, 61, 83, 149, 168
    feminist pedagogy and, 167, 169
    narrative and, 69
    personal, 47, 83, 169–170
    relationship to text, 64, 68, 72,
       83, 169–170, 177
    relocation and, 167, 169
    transcript data and, 158

factual genres, 79, 81, 83, 84
feminism, 151, 168
    autobiographical writing and,
       155–156, 178
    liberal, 153
    multiplicity of, 151, 155
    radical, 153
    three tier stage of, 153–155
    universal category of woman
       and, 156
feminist
    composition, 85, 168–169
    critique, 170
    identity within university, 41–
       42

pedagogy, 167–170
poetics, 114
poststructuralism. *See* feminist
    poststructuralism
theories of language, 152–154
feminist poststructuralism, 58, 62,
    145, 149–157, 172, 176, 180
    distance learning and, 149
    See also poststructuralism

gender
    construction of, 32
    subjectivity and, 151–154, 175,
       180
gendered text, 28, 30–31, 153–154
genre, 29, 31–33, 82, 83, 85–86,
    92, 110, 172, 179
    critical literacy and, 92
    factual, 83–84
    feminist critique of, 85
    genre-process debate, 21–22
    genre specific strategies, 175
    personal/factual binary, 79,
       83–84
    prescriptive nature of, 94
    procedural, 30–31
    typology of, 83–84
    writing conference critique and,
       63

hupomnemata, 49–50

journal writing, 124–127

labour
    relationship to voice, 177–178
language
    alienation of women and, 153
    as neutral communication, 126
    as social semiotic, 25–26, 51–54
    as socially and culturally
       located, 128
liberatory pedagogies, 46–47, 181
linguistics
    critical, 114
    difficulties with critical use,
       123

determinism, 153
metalanguage, 79, 87, 105,
    114–115, 116, 175, 179, 180
structuralist, 113, 114, 123
systemic functional. *See* sys-
    temic functional linguistics
literacy, critical. *See* critical
    literacy

memory work, 58, 155
metalanguage
    linguistic, 101–106
    poststructuralist, 87–91
    spatialised, 87, 91–101
modality, 101, 102–103, 132–134,
    181. *See also* systemic
    functional linguistics
multiliteracies, 54
multiple voices, 43, 176, 180

narrative, 44–45, 77, 83, 156, 170,
    177, 178, 180
    autobiographical, 144
    collective biography, 4–5
    counternarrative, 76, 77, 175,
        180
    criticism, 155, 156
    dominant, 57, 72–75
    experience and, 69
    autoethnography and, 4
    research method, 158
    spatialisation and, 2–3, 5
    story and, 46
    textual orientation, 177–178
nominalisation, 101, 103–106, 107,
    124, 134. *See also* systemic
    functional linguistics

passive voice, 125, 126
personal
    academic spaces and, 137
    as motivation, 73–74
    as textual representation, 28,
        29, 59, 60, 64, 116, 126, 171,
        177
    critical discourse analysis and,
        109

experience, 47, 83, 169–170
genre, 83, 84
interface with the social, 49
metaphoric relationship to
    stories, 176
notebooks. *See* hupomnemata
relationship to private, 50
relocation and, 8, 33, 47, 76
subjectivity and, 47–48
voice, 28, 63, 168, 176, 177
writing. *See* personal writing
See also self
personal writing, 79, 82–83, 84,
    156, 157, 170, 171, 172, 176,
    177, 183
    discourse analysis and, 115–
        116, 120
    limitations in school context,
        134
    See also autobiography
poetry, 156
    construction from transcripts,
        159–160
    See also transcript poem
politics, 22, 48, 76, 134, 154, 180,
    182–183
    of difference, 156
    of feminism within the univer-
        sity, 41–42
    of location, 9
    of selection, 174
    of space, 122, 171
positioning, 10, 58, 61, 111, 131,
    180
poststructuralism, 5–6, 47–48, 64,
    69, 74, 91, 112, 113, 115,
    152, 158, 171, 176, 178, 179
    feminist. *See* feminist post-
        structuralism
poststructuralist
    data collection, 10–11
    metalanguage, 79, 87–88, 116
power, 53, 61, 68, 73, 74, 79, 82,
    83, 85, 89–91, 102–103, 109,
    111, 112, 114, 115, 128, 130,
    133–134, 152, 168, 178, 179,
    182

procedural genre
  characteristics of, 30–31
process writing, 9–15, 20, 28, 33,
    61–62, 73, 84, 110, 168, 172,
    179
  feminist pedagogy and, 168

relocation, 1, 173, 176
  argument and, 83
  experience and, 167, 169
  life as, 5–9
  personal, 8, 33, 47, 76
  power and, 168
  real purposes for writing and,
    73
  subjectivity and, 51
  student writer and, 106
  transformation and, 54
  voice and social transformation
    and, 47
  writing conference and, 14–15,
    61–62
  writing workshop and, 116
representation, 48, 61, 68–69, 73,
    76, 111, 171, 177, 180, 181
  social semiotic theory of, 51–53
  writer as signmaker, 51–53

self
  appropriation and, 50
  care for, 49
  government of, 48–49
  presentation in text, 86, 102
  relationship to voice, 44, 177
  writing and, 3, 5, 28, 38–39, 60,
    169, 173, 181
  See also personal
self-writing, 48–51, 85
  voice and, 50
signs
  meaning and, 51, 53
  theory of representation and,
    51–53
  writing workshop and, 60
situated voice, 43, 44, 176
spatialisation, 70, 86–87, 171, 178
  argument and, 95–97

narrative and, 2–3, 5
voice and, 36
spatialised metalanguage. See
  metalanguage
story
  as fiction, 137, 155, 156, 167,
    170
  as learned cultural practice, 46
  as metaphor of the personal,
    176
  metaphors of, 45
  movement from voice, 44–46
  narrative and, 46, 177
  nature of, 45–46
  poststructural analysis and, 57,
    64
  textual orientation, 45, 177–178
storylines, 57, 68, 69, 73, 153
  ageing, 65–67
  birthing, 144–145, 146–147
  death, 56–57, 74–75
  family politics, 117–118
  female circumcision, 138–144
  good wife, 70–71, 118–119
student
  as researcher, 34, 110, 122–123
  voice, 39–42, 46
  writing journals and, 126
subjectivity, 51, 60–61, 83, 89,
    101, 106, 114, 118, 152, 167,
    171, 173, 179, 180
  argument and, 86
  defined, 47–48
  discourse analysis and, 112
  gendered, 151–154, 175, 180
  identity and, 53
  personal, 47–48
  relocation and, 51
  telling facts and, 72
  writing and, 53–54, 60, 167
  writing pedagogies and, 53–54,
    61, 181–182
systemic functional linguistics,
    25, 29, 32, 33, 101, 113–115,
    178
  absence of social critique in,
    33, 114

modality, 101, 102–103, 132–134, 181
nominalisation, 101, 103–106, 107, 124, 134
theme, 101–103
transitivity, 18, 19, 23–24, 30

teacher's
essay comments as text, 88–89
questions, and writing conference, 14, 63–64, 68–70, 74, 116, 150, 180
voice, 42–43
telling facts, 69, 70, 72
textuality
metaphors of, 46, 177, 178
theme analysis, 101–103. *See also* systemic functional linguistics
transcript poem, 158–159, 175
construction of, 159–160
example of, 160–166
transformation, 36, 47, 59, 73, 169
relocation and, 54
writing and, 47, 54, 158, 177
transitivity, 18, 19, 23–24, 30. *See also* systemic functional linguistics

voice
active, 125
adequacy of metaphor, 43–44, 176
appropriation and, 38, 50
as participation, 38–39
as project, 43–44
authentic, 61, 134
authenticity and, 43
conceptions of, 37
female, 137
labour and 177–178
movement to story from, 44–46
multiple, 43, 176, 180
narrative, 48
passive, 125, 126
poststructuralist critique of, 38–40

power and, 40–42, 168
relationship to self, 44, 177
relocation and, 47
self-writing and, 50
situated, 43, 44, 176
social transformation and, 47
spatialisation and, 36
speech and sound metaphors and, 45
stories and, 44–46
student, 39–42
teacher's, 42–43
writing workshop and, 36, 38–42

workbench metaphor, 62–63, 91
See also clay work
writing
absences and, 65, 116, 180–181
argumentative. *See* argument
as crafting, 167, 178, 182
as design for subjectivity, 48, 53–54, 59–60, 72, 86, 167, 181–182
as political project, 73–77, 171–185
as selection, 68, 71–72
as social action, 3, 4, 119, 166, 180, 182
as therapy, 59, 64, 167, 181
autobiographical. *See* autobiography
collaborative, 168
conference. *See* writing conference
critical models, absence of, 109–110
cross genre, 155–156, 175
cultural production and, 72
detail in, 68–72
disruptive, 156–158, 170, 175
distance learning and, 149–151, 155
emotion and, 167
in examinations, 94–95, 99
male/female binary and, 154
personal. *See* personal writing
real purposes and, 73

writing *(continued)*
  self and, 3, 5, 28, 38–39, 60,
    169, 173, 181
  student journals and, 126
  third person and, 68, 126, 181
  transformative power and, 47,
    54, 158, 177
  voice and, 28, 36–46
  See also writing pedagogies
writing conference, 14, 27–28,
    61–62
  as interview, 63
  genre critique and, 63
  political purposes and, 73–74
poststructural influence on, 62,
    64–65
  relocation and, 14–15, 61–62
  student's questions of, 119

teacher's questions and, 14,
    63–64, 68–70, 74, 116, 150,
    180
  teleconferencing and, 150
  telling facts and, 69, 70, 72
  workbench metaphor and 62–63
writing pedagogies, 2–3, 8
  curriculum debates and, 22–23
  linguistics and, 33
  representation and, 53–54
  student teachers and, 121–123
  subjectivity and, 53–54, 61,
    181–182
  writing conference and, 14,
    27–28
writing workshop, 173, 181
  text production and, 60–61
  voice and, 36, 38–42, 50